Mastering Ruby on Rails

Mastering Computer Science
Series Editor: Sufyan bin Uzayr

Mastering Ruby on Rails: A Beginner's Guide
Mathew Rooney and Madina Karybzhanova

Mastering Sketch: A Beginner's Guide
Mathew Rooney and Md Javed Khan

Mastering C#: A Beginner's Guide
Mohamed Musthafa MC, Divya Sachdeva, and Reza Nafim

Mastering GitHub Pages: A Beginner's Guide
Sumanna Kaul and Shahryar Raz

Mastering Unity: A Beginner's Guide
Divya Sachdeva and Aruqqa Khateib

Mastering Unreal Engine: A Beginner's Guide
Divya Sachdeva and Aruqqa Khateib

For more information about this series, please visit: https://www.routledge.com/Mastering-Computer-Science/book-series/MCS

The "Mastering Computer Science" series of books are authored by the Zeba Academy team members, led by Sufyan bin Uzayr.

Zeba Academy is an EdTech venture that develops courses and content for learners primarily in STEM fields, and offers education consulting to Universities and Institutions worldwide. For more info, please visit https://zeba.academy

Mastering Ruby on Rails

A Beginner's Guide

Edited by Sufyan bin Uzayr

CRC Press
Taylor & Francis Group
Boca Raton London New York

CRC Press is an imprint of the
Taylor & Francis Group, an **informa** business

First edition published 2022
by CRC Press

6000 Broken Sound Parkway NW, Suite 300, Boca Raton, FL 33487-2742

and by CRC Press
2 Park Square, Milton Park, Abingdon, Oxon, OX14 4RN

CRC Press is an imprint of Taylor & Francis Group, LLC

© 2022 Sufyan bin Uzayr

ISBN: 978-1-032-13509-0 (hbk)
ISBN: 978-1-032-13507-6 (pbk)
ISBN: 978-1-003-22960-5 (ebk)

DOI: 10.1201/9781003229605

Typeset in Minion
by KnowledgeWorks Global Ltd.

Contents

About the Editor

Sufyan bin Uzayr is a writer, coder, and entrepreneur with more than a decade of experience in the industry. He has authored several books in the past, pertaining to a diverse range of topics, ranging from History to Computers/IT.

Sufyan is the Director of Parakozm, a multinational IT company specializing in EdTech solutions. He also runs Zeba Academy, an online learning and teaching vertical with a focus on STEM fields.

Sufyan specializes in a wide variety of technologies, such as JavaScript, Dart, WordPress, Drupal, Linux, and Python. He holds multiple degrees, including ones in Management, IT, Literature, and Political Science.

Sufyan is a digital nomad, dividing his time between four countries. He has lived and taught in universities and educational institutions around the globe. Sufyan takes a keen interest in technology, politics, literature, history, and sports, and in his spare time, he enjoys teaching coding and English to young students.

Learn more at sufyanism.com.

## CHAPTER 1

Introduction to Ruby on Rails

IN THIS CHAPTER

➢ Getting to know the history of Ruby on Rails

➢ Learning about Ruby on Rails key features and technical requirements

➢ Understanding framework's installation procedure

Ruby on Rails is a server-side web application development framework written in Ruby language. Ruby on Rails' emergence was greatly influenced web app development, through innovative attributes such as seamless database table creations, migrations, and scaffolding of views to support rapid application development. Ruby on Rails is known for its model–view–controller (MVC) framework,

DOI: 10.1201/9781003229605-1   **1**

providing default structures for a database, a web service, and web pages. It encourages and eases the use of web standards such as JSON or XML for data transfer and HTML, CSS, and JavaScript for user interfacing.

Ruby on Rails' influence on other web frameworks is rather apparent today, with many frameworks in other languages borrowing its ideas, including Django in Python, Catalyst in Perl, Laravel, CakePHP and Yii in PHP, Grails in Groovy, Phoenix in Elixir, Play in Scala, and Sails.js in Node.js. Some currently popular sites that use Ruby on Rails include Airbnb, Crunchbase, and Bloomberg.

WHAT IS RUBY AND RUBY ON RAILS?

Since Ruby on Rails is written in Ruby, it is only fair to review the history of Ruby development first. Ruby is a high-level, interpreted, general-purpose programming language. It was designed and created in 1993, conceived in a discussion about the possibility of founding a new object-oriented scripting language between Yukihiro Matsumoto ("Matz") and his colleague. Matz stated in his ruby-talk:00382 blog that he knew Perl but did not like it very much since it was too plain for him. He also discussed that he knew Python but did not like its basic operational principles.

At that point of time Matz was simply looking for a language perfect for his needs that was:

- Syntactically uncomplicated

- Truly object-oriented

- Included iterators and closures

- Had exception handling

- Offered garbage collection
- Was portable

Having looked around and not found a language appropriate for his requirements, Yukihiro Matsumoto decided to create his own. After spending several months writing an interpreter, Matz finally presented the first public version of Ruby (0.95) to various Japanese local newsgroups in December 1995.

Ruby ended up being everything that other languages could not offer: dynamically typed and using garbage collection with just-in-time compilation. Moreover, it supports multiple programming paradigms, including procedural, object-oriented, and functional programming. Ruby was mostly influenced by Perl, Smalltalk, Eiffel, Ada, BASIC, and Lisp, according to its creator.

Ruby is also said to follow the principle of least astonishment (POLA), meaning that the language is set to behave in such a way as to reduce confusion for experienced users. Matsumoto shared that his primary design goal was to create a language that he enjoyed using by minimizing programmer routine and possible disarray.

Ruby was intentionally made purely object-oriented, meaning that every value it has stands as an object, including classes and instances of types that many other languages designate as primitives (such as integers, Booleans, and "null"). At the same time, variables always hold references to objects. Every function is treated as a method, and methods are always called on an object. Methods defined at the top-level scope become methods of the Object class. Since this class is an ancestor of every other class, such methods can be called on any object. It is also important to remember that rules applying to objects apply to the entire Ruby. They are also visible in all scopes, effectively serving as "global" procedures.

Additionally, Ruby supports inheritance with dynamic dispatch, mixins, and singleton methods (belonging to, and defined for, a single instance rather than being defined on the class). Though Ruby does not support multiple inheritances, classes can import modules as mixins.

Ruby has previously been described as a multi-paradigm programming language. Basically, that means it allows procedural programming (defining functions/variables outside classes to make them part of the root), with object-orientation (everything is an object) or functional programming (supporting anonymous functions, closures, and continuations; statements all have values, and functions return the last evaluation). It has support for introspection, reflection, and metaprogramming, as well as support for interpreter-based threads. Ruby also has the capacity for dynamic typing and supports parametric polymorphism (a programming technique that enables the generic definition of functions and types).

Since its public release in 1995, Ruby has gained devoted coders worldwide. In 2006, Ruby achieved mass praise. Active user groups were particularly fond of Ruby due to the following key features:

- **Flexibility:** Ruby is a flexible language as you can easily delete, redefine, or add existing parts to it. It allows its users to freely change and advance its essential parts as they wish. With that, Ruby tries not to restrict the coder.

To illustrate with an example, addition is performed with the plus (+) operator. However, if you would rather use the readable word plus, you could add such a method to Ruby's built-in Numeric class:

```
class Numeric
  def plus(x)
    self.+(x)
end
end
y = 5.plus 6
# y is now equal to 11
```

At the same time, Ruby's operators could be applied as syntactic links for methods. If necessary, you can redefine them as well.

• **The expressive capacity of Blocks:** Ruby's block could also be the reason for its great flexibility. A programmer can attach a closure to any method, regulating how that method should act. The closure is called a block and has become one of the most popular features for newcomers to Ruby from other imperative languages like PHP or Visual Basic. Blocks are mainly inspired by functional languages and could be demonstrated in the following manner:

```
search_engines =
  %w[Google Yahoo MSN].map do |engine|
    "http://www." + engine.downcase +
".com"
  end
```

In the above code, the block is whatever you see inside the do … end construct. The map method applies the block to the provided list of words. Many other methods in Ruby leave an open space for a coder to insert their own block to fill in the details of what that method should achieve.

• **Mixins:** Unlike many object-oriented languages, Ruby supports single inheritance only. To put it simply, Ruby has classes as well as modules. And a module has methods but no instances. Instead, a module can be mixed into a class, which adds the method of that module to the class. It is similar to regular inheritance but much more flexible.

To illustrate, any class which executes the method can mix-in the Enumerable module, which adds a pile of methods that use each for looping:

```
class MyArray
   include Enumerable
end
```

• **Visual appearance:** While Ruby often applies very limited punctuation and typically prefers English keywords, some punctuation is still used to decorate Ruby. At the same time Ruby needs no variable declarations since it uses simple naming conventions to mark the scope of variables:

```
var could be a local variable.
@var is an instance variable.
$var is a global variable.
```

These signs advance readability by letting the programmer easily identify the roles of each variable. It also becomes unnecessary to insert a tedious self, prepended to every instance item.

- **Dynamic typing and duck typing:** It has previously been stated that Ruby is a dynamic programming language. Meaning that Ruby programs are not compiled—all class, module, and method definition are built by the code only. This is dynamic typing.

  At the same time, Ruby variables are loosely typed language, which means any variable can hold any type of object. When a method is called on an object, Ruby only looks up at the name irrespective of the type of object. This is duck typing. It lets you take classes that pretend to be other classes.

- **Variable constants:** In Ruby, constants do not actually act as constants. If an already initialized constant will be edited in a script, it will simply result in a warning but will not terminate your program.

- **Naming conventions:** Ruby has particular naming conventions for its variable, method, constant, and class:

  - **Constant:** Starts with a capital letter.

  - **Global variable:** Starts with a dollar sign ($).

  - **Instance variable:** Starts with a (@) sign.

  - **Class variable:** Starts with a (@@) sign.

  - **Method name:** Allowed to start with a capital letter.

  - **Keyword arguments:** like Python, Ruby methods can be defined using keyword arguments.

- **Method names:** Methods are permitted to end with a question mark (?) or exclamation mark (!). Normally, methods that answer questions end with question marks, and methods that identify that method can change the state of the object end with an exclamation mark.

- **Singleton methods:** Ruby singleton methods are per-object methods. They are only available on the object you determined it on.

- **Missing method:** In case a method gets lost, Ruby calls the method_missing method with the name of the lost method.

- **Statement delimiters:** It is a rule that multiple statements in a single line must hold semi-colon in between but not at the end of a line.

- **Keywords:** Ruby has a special set of words that are considered "reserved" meaning that they should not be used when naming variables or methods. The following list displays all Ruby reserved words:[1]

  1. **BEGIN:** Code, enclosed in { and }, to run before the program runs.

  2. **END:** Code, enclosed in { and }, to run when the program ends.

  3. **alias:** Creates an alias for an existing method, operator, or global variable.

---

[1] http://www.java2s.com/Code/Ruby/Language-Basics/Rubysreservedwords. htm, Java

4. **and:** Logical operator; same as && except and has lower precedence.

5. **begin:** Begins a code block or group of statements; closes with end.

6. **break:** Terminates a while or until loop or a method inside a block.

7. **\case:** Compares an expression with a matching when clause; closes with end.

8. **Class:** Defines a class; closes with end.

9. **def:** Defines a method; closes with end.

10. **defined?:** Determines if a variable, method, super method, or block exists.

11. **do:** Begins a block and executes code in that block; closes with end.

12. **else:** Executes if previous conditional, in if, elsif, unless, or when, is not true.

13. **elsif:** Executes if previous conditional, in if or elsif, is not true.

14. **end:** Ends a code block (group of statements) starting with begin, def, do, if, etc.

15. **ensure:** Always executes at block termination; use after last rescue.

16. **false:** Logical or Boolean false, an instance of FalseClass. (See true.)

17. **for:** Begins a for loop; used within.

18. **if:** Executes code block if true. Closes with end.

19. **module:** Defines a module; closes with end.

20. **next:** Jumps before a loop's conditional.

21. **nil:** Empty, uninitialized variable, or invalid, but not the same as zero; object of NilClass.

22. **not:** Logical operator; same as !.

23. **or:** Logical operator; same as || except or has lower precedence.

24. **redo:** Jumps after a loop's conditional.

25. **rescue:** Evaluates an expression after an exception is raised; used before ensure.

26. **retry:** Repeats a method call outside of rescue; jumps to the top of block (begin) if inside rescue.

27. **return:** Returns a value from a method or block. Maybe omitted.

28. **self:** Current object (invoked by a method).

29. **super:** Calls method of the same name in the superclass. The superclass is the parent of this class.

30. **then:** A continuation for if, unless, and when. Maybe omitted.

31. **true:** Logical or Boolean true, an instance of TrueClass.

32. **undef:** Makes a method in the current class undefined.

33. **unless:** Executes code block if the conditional statement is false.

34. **until:** Executes code block while conditional statement is false.

35. **when:** Starts a clause (one or more) under case.

36. **while:** Executes code while the conditional statement is true.

37. **yield:** Executes the block passed to the method.

38. _ _**FILE**_ _: Name of the current source file.

39. _ _**LINE**_ _: Number of the current line in the current source file.

- **Case Sensitive:** It is worth noting that Ruby is a case-sensitive language. Lowercase letters and uppercase letters are different.

  Although we have many reasons to use Ruby, there are still a few drawbacks as well that you might have to consider before implementing Ruby:

  - **Performance Issues:** Although it opposes Perl and Python, it is still an interpreted language that cannot be compared with high-level programming languages like C or C++.

  - **Threading model:** Ruby does not utilize native threads. In Ruby threads are simulated in rather than running as native OS threads.

Sample Ruby Code to print "Hello Ruby" is quite straightforward:

```
# The Hello Class
class Hello
    def initialize( name )
      @name = name.capitalize
    end

    def salute
      puts "Hello #{@name}!"
    end
    end

# Create a new object
h = Hello.new("Ruby")

# Output "Hello Ruby!"
h.salute
Output - This will produce the
following result -
Hello Ruby!
```

Another important thing about Ruby worth mentioning is a program called Embedded Ruby (ERB). Ruby provides an ERB written by Seki Masatoshi that allows you to put Ruby codes inside an HTML file. ERB reads along, word for word, and then at a certain point, when it encounters a Ruby code embedded in the document, it starts running the Ruby code.

There are two things to take care of when preparing an ERB document:

If you want some Ruby code executed, enclose it between <% and %>. If you want the result of the code execution to be printed out, as a part of the output, enclose the code between <%= and %>. To illustrate with an example:[2]

```
<% page_title = "Demonstration of ERB" %>
<% salutation = "Dear programmer," %>
<html>

    <head>
        <title><%= page_title %></title>
    </head>

    <body>
        <p><%= salutation %></p>
        <p>This is an example of how ERB
fills out a template.</p>
    </body>

</html>
```

Now, run the program using the command-line utility erb.

```
tp> erb erbdemo.rb
```

This will produce the following result—

```
<html>
    <head>
        <title>Demonstration of ERb</title>
    </head>
    <body>
        <p>Dear programmer,</p>
        <p>This is an example of how ERb
fills out a template.</p>
    </body>

</html>
```

---

[2] https://www.ruby-lang.org/en/about/, Ruby

Overall, Ruby is a great language. Matz wanted a programming language that catered to his needs, so he created one. This inspiring example sends a motivating message to the software development community—if you cannot find something that you like, just create it yourself. Until 2004, Ruby was not widely popular across Europe or the United States. However, because of its impressive capabilities and a large number of supported platforms, Ruby slowly but surely exponentially grew the number of its followers. The real spike of interest in Ruby was provoked by the development of Ruby on Rails—a framework for producing web applications.

Ruby on Rails was created by a Danish programmer, David Heinemeier Hansson. In 1999, Hansson founded and built a Danish online gaming website and community called Daily Rush, which he owned until 2001. After collaborating with Jason Fried to work on PHP coding, Hansson was hired by Fried to build a web-based project management tool, which ultimately became 37signals Basecamp software as a service product. In order to advance the development process, Hansson used the then-obscure Ruby programming language to code a custom web framework. He released the framework separately from the project management tool in 2004 as the open-source project called "Ruby on Rails." A year after that, in 2005, Hansson was recognized by Google and O'Reilly with the "Hacker of the Year" award for his creation of Ruby on Rails.

Hansson first released Rails as open source in July 2004 but did not share the commit rights until February 2005. Soon after, in August 2006, the Apple company announced that it would ship Ruby on Rails with Mac OS X v10.5 "Leopard."

On March 15, 2009, Rails version 2.3 was released. It was a notable version as it included major new developments in templates, engines, and nested model forms.

On December 23, 2008, another web application framework called Merb was launched. Rails announced that it would work with the Merb project to incorporate the best ideas of MVC Merb into Rails 3. As a result of such collaboration, all the unnecessary duplication of codes in both frameworks were eliminated. The full Ruby version history could be viewed in the list below:[3]

Version	Release Date
1.0	December 13, 2005
1.2	January 19, 2007
2.0	December 7, 2007
2.1	June 1, 2008
2.2	November 21, 2008
2.3	March 16, 2009
3.0	August 29, 2010
3.1	August 31, 2011
3.2	January 20, 2012
4.0	June 25, 2013
4.1	April 8, 2014
4.2	December 19, 2014
5.0	June 30, 2016
5.1	May 10, 2017
5.2	April 9, 2018
6.0	August 16, 2019
6.1	December 9, 2020

---

[3] https://weblog.rubyonrails.org/releases/, Ruby on Rails

The Rails philosophy is founded on two major guiding principles:[4]

1. **Don't Repeat Yourself:** DRY is a principle of software development that could be described as

   Every piece of knowledge must have a single, straightforward, authoritative representation within a system.

   By not scripting the same information over and over again, Rails code looks more maintainable, more extensible, and uncomplicated.

2. **Convention Over Configuration:** Rails offers you some options from which you can choose the best way to do many things in a web application, and defaults to this set of conventions, rather than require you to determine specific rules and tasks through endless configuration files.

One could guess that Rails could be quite an opinionated software. It makes the assumption that there is the most suitable way to achieve things, and it is designed to encourage that way—and in some instances to discourage alternatives. If you stick with "The Rails Way" you will probably discover a significant increase in productivity. On the other hand, if you persist in bringing old practices from other languages to your Rails development, and continuing to apply patterns you learned elsewhere, you may have a less smooth experience.

---

[4] https://guides.rubyonrails.org/getting_started.html, Ruby on Rails

Experienced programmers choose Ruby on Rails because:

- It allows them to launch a faster web application.

- Helps with maintaining and avoiding issues with stuff migration.

- They can easily update their apps with the latest functionality.

- It uses Metaprogramming techniques (by which computer programs have the ability to treat other programs as their data) to write programs.

You can use Ruby on Rails application in various areas of web development like long-term projects that require large transformations, or in the project that has heavy traffic, or to produce a short prototype or minimum viable product (MVP), or in a project that requires wide range of complex functions.

MAJOR FEATURES

As you might know, most programming languages like Java, HTML, or CSS do not cover the front and back end. They either cater only to the back end or the front end, but Ruby on Rails could easily be used for both the front and back end, acting like a complete set to develop a web application. Some of the most important features of Ruby on Rails are:

1. **MVC Architecture:** Ruby on Rails uses MVC architecture that consists of three key components— model, view, and controller. The model is used to carry on the interrelation between object and database.

The view acts as a template that is applied to build the data users utilize to create web applications. The controller is activated to merge the model and view together.

2. **Active Records:** The active record framework was first introduced in Ruby on Rails. It could be described as a powerful library that allows the developer to design the database interactive queries.

3. **Built-in Testing:** Ruby on Rails runs its own set of tests that will examine and evaluate your code. This feature alone saves a considerable amount of time and effort.

4. **Programming Language:** The basic syntax of Ruby on Rails is simple because the syntax of the Ruby programming language is close to English, so it is easier to structure your thinking and writing it into code.

5. **Convention Over Configuration:** In Ruby on Rails, a programmer can only specify the unconventional aspects of the application, leaving the conventional items to the language default settings.

6. **Scaffolding:** Ruby on rails provides a scaffolding feature in which the developer is encouraged to define how the application database should work. Once the work of the application database is defined, the framework shall automatically generate the required code according to the given definition. This technique permits the automatic creation of interfaces.

While you are developing Rails applications, especially those which are mostly providing you with a simple interface to data in a database, it can often be beneficial to follow the scaffold method. Scaffolding also provides additional benefits such as:

- Quickly getting code in front of your users for feedback.

- Learning how Rails works by looking at the generated code.

- Using scaffolding as a foundation to jump-start your app development.

At the same time there are some incredibly useful advantages of Ruby on Rails one should now:

- **Tooling:** Rails provides tooling that helps users to deliver more features in less time.

- **Code Quality:** Rails code quality is significantly higher than of PHP or NodeJS equivalents.

- **Test Automation:** The Rails community is big into test automation and general code testing.

- **Large Community:** Rails have a large and supportive community of users, developers, and experts.

- **Productivity:** Ruby is incredibly fast from another language, making its productivity higher than in any other average programming language.

Nevertheless, there are certain disadvantages of Ruby on Rails that need to be mentioned such as:

- **Runtime Speed:** The run time speed of Ruby on Rails is slow compared to Node.Js and Golang operational capacity.

- **Lack of Flexibility:** As we know that Ruby on Rails is perfect for standard web applications due to its established dependency between components and models. Yet when it comes to adding unique functionality and customization in apps, it could be challenging.

- **Boot Speed:** The boot speed is another drawback of Rails. Due to the dependence upon the number of gem dependencies and files, it takes some time to start, which can seriously limit the developer's performance.

- **Multithreading:** Ruby on Rails supports multithreading, but some IO libraries do not support multithreading because they prefer to make use of the global interpreter lock. It basically means that if you are not careful enough, your request will get queued up behind the active requests, and you might experience certain performance issues.

- **Active Record:** Due to the access use of Active records in the Ruby on Rails their hard dependency, the domain becomes tightly coupled to your persistence mechanism.

Most essential tools that have made Rails so widely popular include the following:

- **AJAX Library:** Ajax stands for Asynchronous JavaScript and XML. Ajax is not a single technology but rather a combination of several technologies. It successfully incorporates the following:

  - XHTML for the markup of web pages

  - CSS for the styling

  - Dynamic display and interaction using the DOM

  - Data manipulation and interchange using XML

  - Data retrieval using XMLHttpRequest

  - JavaScript as the glue that meshes all this together

Ajax enables you to retrieve data for a web page without having to refresh the entire page's contents. In the basic web architecture, the user has to click a link or submit a form. The form is submitted to the server, which then sends back a response. The response is then displayed for the user on a new page.

When you interact with an Ajax-powered web page, it loads an Ajax engine in the background. The engine is scripted in JavaScript, and its responsibility is to both communicate with the webserver and offer the results to the user. When you submit data using an Ajax-powered form, the server returns an HTML item that holds the server's response and presents only the new or modified data instead of refreshing the entire page.

- **Symbol Garbage Collector:** Omitting unnecessary symbols could potentially result in minor attacks on your system. The symbol garbage collector combines all the symbols which prevent your system from those attacks.

- **Module #prepend:** This option allows you to insert a module in front of the class it was prepended.

- **Keyword Arguments:** Rails support keyword arguments that help to control memory consumption by Rails applications.

- **Action Mailer:** New methods deliver_now or deliver_later are offered instead of #deliver and #deliver!.

- **Action View:** Helper methods like content_tag_for and div_for were eliminated from the core and placed in a separate gem.

- **Turbolinks:** Sometimes web pages reload very slowly because it requests a full page from the server. Turbolinks 3 reloads only the content of the body and not the whole page.

- **Rails Application Programming Interface (API):** This option enables you to generate API and clean all the middleware that an application does not require.

- **Render From Anywhere:** In earlier versions, you had to use gem render_anywhere to render views outside the controller. Starting from Rails 5, you can render your views from anywhere.

- **Rake Command:** Rails 5 provides you a feature that allows you to restart all your apps with the rake restart command.

- **Customized URL:** Search engine-friendly URLs can be developed or customized in Rails.

- **Action Text:** Perhaps another notable item for many applications that play with WYSIWYG editors is the addition of support for Trix editor natively starting from Rails 6 applications. Most WYSIWYG HTML editors are enormous in scope—each browser's rendering has its own set of bugs and quirks, and JavaScript developers are left to deal with the inconsistencies. Trix organized these inconsistencies by regulating content editable as an I/O device. Thus, when input makes its way to the editor, Trix converts that input into an editing operation on its internal document model, then re-renders that document back into the editor. This gives Trix complete control over all of the processes. Its installation into Rails is pretty straightforward:

```
rails action_text:install
# app/models/message.rb
class Message < ApplicationRecord
  has_rich_text :content
end
```

- **Security:** No serious upgrade is ever complete without a few necessary security enhancements. And as one might expect, Rails do not disappoint on the security front, either. The first notable security upgrade in Rails 6 is the inclusion of support for

Host Authorization. Host Authorization stands for a new middleware that guards against DNS rebinding attacks by explicitly allowing you to whitelist some hosts for your application and preventing Host header attacks. What this means is that you can determine the amount and quality of hosts that can access your applications.

Another significant security upgrade is meant to thwart attacks that try and copy the signed/encrypted value of a cookie and apply it as the value of another cookie. It does so by collecting the cookie names in the purpose field, which is then signed/encrypted along with the cookie value. Then, on the server-side read, you confirm the cookie names and discard any unwanted cookies. In order to use this feature, you just need to enable action_dispatch.use_cookies_ with_metadata which scripts cookies with the new purpose and expiry metadata embedded.

- **Webpack as the Default Bundler:** As the basic standard with many modern JavaScript frameworks for front-end development, Rails 6 has added Webpack as the default JavaScript bundler through the webpacker gem, removing the Rails Asset Pipeline. This is a relatively straightforward addition, and there is no need to go into much detail now. Suffice to say that Webpack was brought to propose certain advancements to overworked front-end developers.

Since the 5.2 version of Rails, credentials have been named a new "Rails way" to deal with sensitive information with a promise to get rid of. env files once and for all.

With credentials, encrypted keys for third-party services can be examined directly into the source control. Yet until now, Rails used the same encrypted file for all environments, which made operating with different keys in development and production slightly challenging, especially when managing big projects and legacy code.

In Rails 6, this has finally been solved with support for per-environment credentials. In fact, Rails 6 could be viewed as a major update, though few would regard it as a game-changer. Since Ruby on Rails has been around for a long time now, few people expect extraordinary changes, but its sixth incarnation brings a lot to the community.

Some features that came with Rails 6 might seem like minor corrections, while others have the potential to save a lot of development time, improve security, and flexibility. The bottom line here is that Rails is a mature programming language, a lot of developers remain enthusiastic about its potential, and with the release of Rails 6, it only got better.

Like other web frameworks, Ruby on Rails applies the MVC pattern to organize application programming. In a default configuration, a model in the Ruby on Rails framework maps to a table in a database and to a Ruby file. For instance, a model class User will usually be identified in the file "user.rb" in the app/models directory and linked to the table "users" in the database. While developers are free to disregard this particular convention and select differing names for their models, files, and database table, this is not a prevalent practice and is usually discouraged in accordance with the "convention-over-configuration" philosophy we have previously mentioned.

A controller is a server-side unit of Rails that reacts to external requests from the webserver to the application, by deciding which view file to render. The controller may also have to query one or more models for general data and pass these on to the view. For instance, in an airline reservation system, a controller executing a flight-search feature would have to query a model representing individual flights to find flights matching the search, and might also need to query models representing airports and airlines to look for related secondary data. The controller would then pass some subset of the flight data to the corresponding view, which would hold a mixture of static HTML and logic that apply to the flight data to produce an HTML document that consists of a table with one row per flight. A controller, therefore, can provide one or more actions. In Ruby on Rails, an action stands for a basic component that states how to react to a particular external web browser request. It is also important to keep in mind that the controller/action will be accessible for external web requests only if a corresponding route is outlined to it. Rails encourages developers to use RESTful routes, which include actions such as create, new, edit, update, destroy, show, and index. These features of incoming requests/routes to controller actions can be easily set up in the routes.rb configuration file. At the same time, a view in the default configuration of Rails is an erb file, which could be reviewed and converted to HTML at run-time. Alternatively, many other templating systems can be used for views.

Since version 2.0, Ruby on Rails offers both HTML and XML as standard output formats. The latter is the facility for RESTful web services. With Rails version 3.1, developers introduced Sass as standard CSS templating. By default, the server still uses ERB in the HTML views, with files having an html.erb extension. In addition, it also supports swapping in alternative templating languages, such as HAML and Mustache.

Ruby on Rails is also noteworthy for its extensive use of the JavaScript libraries Prototype and Script.aculo.us for editing Ajax actions. Ruby on Rails initially applied lightweight SOAP for web services that was later replaced by RESTful web services. Ruby on Rails version 3.0 separated the markup of the page (which determined the structure of the page) from scripting (which decided the functionality or logic of the page). jQuery is fully supported as a replacement for Prototype and is the default JavaScript library since Rails version 3.1, reflecting an industry-wide move toward jQuery. Additionally, CoffeeScript was introduced in the same Rails version 3.1 as the default JavaScript language.

Overall, Ruby on Rails includes great tools that make common development assignments easier, such as scaffolding that can automatically construct some of the models and views necessary for a basic website. Also included are WEBrick, a simple Ruby web server that is packaged with Ruby, and Rake, a build system, distributed as a gem. Together with Ruby on Rails, these tools provide a great development environment.

Typically, Ruby on Rails applications are the most common in the following areas of web development:

- Projects involving a wide range of complex functions;

- Large projects requiring serious transformations;

- Long-term projects that pass through continuous modifications in parameters;

- Projects that have heavy traffic;

- Small, quick projects to develop prototypes and MVPs.

Even though there can be no strict rules here, some developers still do not recommend Ruby on Rails in the following cases:

- No significant modifications in the project;

- A project with limited functionality and uniform operations;

- No need for quick decisions;

- If your project requires low resource consumption.

RAILS VS OTHER FRAMEWORKS

With a variety of programming languages, frameworks, platforms, and development environments, one cannot simply go away without comparing one to the other. Rails is often correlated to other frameworks and environments due to its multi-capacity and flexibility. It tends to completely smudge the line that distinguishes conventional categories like languages and frameworks, providing professionals with a handful of tools to produce scalable and high-quality work.

Ruby on Rails Vs Python

Python is a general-purpose programming language. Some view Python as an all-purpose language that is able to meet any requirements of the coder without having to look for any external tools. In contrast to Python, Ruby on Rails is not a language, it stands out as a framework built upon the Ruby language and explicitly used for web development.

Ruby on Rails Vs PHP

PHP is a language with an object-oriented programming (OOP) structure used for scripting. It is mostly applied in software development, whereas Rails is the framework sought for web development. Same as with Python, this comparison with PHP is not entirely correct since Ruby on Rails is not a language. However, you are very likely going to face many situations where Ruby on Rails and PHP would be applied within the same project.

Ruby on Rails Vs Java

Java is one of the oldest and widely used languages. It is specifically known as a language to develop applications for a variety of operating systems. This technology is especially well-known as being a top language for developing Android apps. In contrast to Java, RoR is commonly used for web development purposes.

Ruby on Rails vs JavaScript

Although they are similarly named, Java and JavaScript are entirely different scripting languages that are created for different purposes. Java's goal is to enable developers to apply the same code on different operating systems without having to modify it much. Yet nowadays, Java applets are getting less popular, with most users preferring Java support disabled in their browsers. On the other hand,

JavaScript is more popular than ever as it runs perfectly well with modern web browsers, especially on mobile.

JavaScript is one of the most widely used front-end programming languages, particularly applied in creating versatile user interfaces for web applications for different devices. Rails and Java share a few basic similarities, but for the most part, they should be perceived as completely different languages. They are both strongly typed and OOP languages, but Rails is an interpreted scripting language while Java is a compiled coding language.

JavaScript and Ruby on Rails are in high demand, and both are viewed as lucrative web development programming languages that each have apparent advantages. At the same time, they go hand in hand really well. That is why, when choosing whether to learn Ruby or JavaScript, you should consider taking the third option and learning both of these computer programming languages.

Ruby on Rails Vs Node.js

Node.js is an open-source platform for implementing JavaScript code server-side, as it was primarily built on the JavaScript runtime. Fundamentally, comparing Node.JS to Rails is like comparing an apple to an orange. Unlike Rails, Node is not a framework but an application runtime environment that allows scripting on the server-side application using JavaScript, while Ruby on Rails is a framework.

Ruby on Rails Vs Ruby

One of the most widely applied programming languages, similar to Java or C, Ruby is an all-purpose language, best-reviewed for its advantages in web programming. On the contrary, Rails is the software library, which broadens Ruby language. And since Ruby and Rails have a longstanding connection, let us observe Ruby with Ruby on Rails in detail starting from the following on-basis table (Table 1.1):[5]

TABLE 1.1   Comparing Ruby Vs Ruby on Rails

Basis	Ruby	Ruby on Rails
Principle	Ruby was founded on the principle of user interface composition.	Ruby on Rails was built on the principles of convention over configuration (CoC) and don't repeat yourself (DRY).
Programmed	Ruby is programmed in the C programming language.	Ruby on Rails is programmed in Ruby language.
Framework	Ruby is not a framework. It is a general-purpose programming language.	Ruby on Rails is a web app development framework.
Inspiration	Ruby took inspiration from Smalltalk and Perl.	Ruby on Rails took inspiration from Django and Laravel of PHP and Python correspondingly.
Applications	Ruby is used to build desktop applications.	For building web applications, Ruby on Rails is used.
Languages used	While building applications, JAVA, C++, and Vb.net are mostly used.	While building applications, XML, JavaScript, CSS, and HTML are commonly used.
Syntax	The syntax of Ruby is much related to Python and Perl.	The syntax of Ruby on Rails is quite similar to Python, Phoenix in Elixir.

---

[5] https://www.monocubed.com/difference-between-ruby-and-ruby-on-rails/, Monocubed

After reviewing the concepts and detailed comparison on Ruby with Rails, let us examine each technology's pros and cons.

Pros and Cons: Ruby

As previously stated, Ruby is an open-source programming language mostly used to develop services and web applications. It has been the best fit for the developers, as it offers an option of blending with other technologies.

Pros

Dependency regulation: Ruby language has a great advantage of automatic regulation of various dependencies. It offers a flawless way to obtain, operate, and execute them. Developers do not need to use any other class directories to manage any added dependencies.

- **Instant gratification:** Ruby is wired to push developers to write codes for forming any large application within a stipulated time, in comparison to other prevalent programming languages that disregard that function.

- **Memory operability:** The management of memory is one of the essential advantages of Ruby, allowing its users to do it physically. While analyzing complex algorithms and using a data structure, developers find this feature to be very helpful.

Cons

- **Shared modifiable state:** In spite of being object-oriented, each object is modifiable in Ruby. Even its originals get an identical state which might issue software bugs that can go to exceptions until the end.

- **Multiple programming pattern:** Ruby supports multiple programming paradigms, which can be an advantage as well as an obstacle. The logic behind it is that developers can be confused to depict the codes while creating a module. This might result in development complications that developers will have to overcome independently and not in a single pattern, which is going to consume much of their time.

- **Syntax complication:** It is not recommended to omit syntax issues, even if the interpreter ignores it due to its massive codebase. Sometimes these concepts get overlooked and the developers tend to avoid such syntaxes.

Pros and Cons: Ruby on Rails

In Ruby and Ruby on Rails, the former language assists in managing diverse databases that split the process between two duplications. This, in turn, supplies services and performance advancement for scaling. Its developers can observe dissimilar database support as an enhancement in constructing their app designs.

Pros

- **Cost-effective:** Rails is an open-source structure, which means that you do not spend any financial resources to get access to its structure. It allows you to implement methods without any extra concepts, so it can save a lot of time.

- **Safe and secure:** A number of great security points are included and authorized within the system. Using Ruby on Rails activates a secure development lifecycle, which is an outstanding security maintenance method.

- **Flexible:** If you hope to attract numerous users to your applications, you must make sure that it can adjust to the necessity of your audience. With amazing features that were listed before, this framework can make the most productive and flexible applications.

Cons

- **Multithreading:** Rails supports Multithreading, which means that if you are not careful, requests could be lined up at the backside of an active request creating additional issues in performance.

- **Ambiguity due to convention:** Apart from the advantages of convention over configuration for beginners, it adds a certain level of ambiguity to skilled developers. For instance, with the nonexistence of configuration files, there is no code, which reveals that the data from a class named "page" is certainly saved to the table defined "chapter."

- **Boot speed:** Most of the programmers who are operating with Ruby on Rails mention that the speed of boot is not up to the anticipation. Due to numerous dependencies and files, it requires considerable time to begin. And because of this, the performance of the developers gets affected.

Hopefully, this section of Ruby on Rails' overview has provided you with enough information about Ruby on Rails as a leading technology and its position in the software development industry.

INSTALLATION AND CONFIGURATION OF RUBY ON RAILS

Before you install Rails, you should check to make sure that your system has the proper prerequisites installed. These include:

- Ruby

- SQLite3

- Node.js

- Yarn

In order to install Ruby, go to https://www.ruby-lang.org/en/downloads/. Once the download is finished, access a command-line prompt. If you are working on macOS you should open Terminal.app; on Windows, choose "Run" from your Start menu and type cmd.exe. Any commands prefaced with a dollar sign $should be run in the command line. Verify that you have a current version of Ruby installed:

```
$ ruby --version
```

Rails requires Ruby version 2.5.0 or later. If the version number returned is less than that number (such as 2.3.7, or 1.8.7), you will need to install a fresh copy of Ruby.

You will also need an installation of the SQLite3 database. Many popular UNIX-like OS ship with an acceptable version of SQLite3. In order to verify that it is correctly installed go to your load PATH:

```
$ sqlite3 --version
```

With that, the program should report its version.

Finally, you'll need Node.js and Yarn installed to manage your application's JavaScript. Find the installation instructions at the Node.js website (https://nodejs.org/en/download/) and verify it is installed correctly with the following command:

```
$ node --version
```

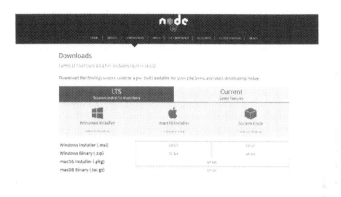

Make sure that the version of your Node.js that should be printed out as output is greater than 8.16.0.

To install Yarn, follow the installation instructions at the Yarn website (https://classic.yarnpkg.com/en/) and run this command to check the available Yarn version:

```
$ yarn --version
```

If it states something like "1.22.0," Yarn has been installed correctly.

In order to install Rails, apply the following gem install command provided by RubyGems in https://rails.github.io/download/:

```
$ gem install rails
```

To verify that you have everything installed correctly, you should be able to run the following:

```
$ rails --version
```

If it displays a result that states—"Rails 6.0.0," then you are ready to continue.

Creating a Sample Blog Application

Rails come with a variety of scripts called generators that are designed to make your development process easier by preparing everything that is necessary to start working on a particular task. One of these is the new application generator, which will provide you with the foundation of a pre-made Rails application so that you do not have to write it yourself.

To use this generator, you should open a terminal and navigate to a directory where you have rights to create files, and run:

```
$ rails new blog
```

This will create a Rails application called Blog in a blog directory and install the necessary gem dependencies. In case you are using Windows Subsystem for Linux, then there are a few limitations on file system notifications that mean you have to disable the spring and listen to gems which you can do by running rails new blog --skip-spring --skip-listen instead. In addition, you can access all of the command-line options that the Rails application generator supports by running rails new --help.

After you create the blog application, you can focus on its folder:

```
$ cd blog
```

This blog directory will display a number of generated files and folders that make up the structure of a Rails application. Most of the work typically takes place in this app folder, but there is also a basic rundown on the function of each of the files and folders that Rails create by default:[6]

- **app/:** Contains the controllers, models, views, helpers, mailers, channels, jobs, and assets for your application.

- **bin/:** Contains the rails script that starts your app and can contain other scripts you use to set up, update, deploy, or run your application.

---

[6] https://guides.rubyonrails.org/getting_started.html, Ruby on Rails

- **config/:** Contains configuration for your application's routes, database, and more.

- **config.ru:** Rack configuration for Rack-based servers used to start the application.

- **db/:** Contains your current database schema, as well as the database migrations.

- **Gemfile.lock:** These files allow you to specify what gem dependencies are needed for your Rails application. These files are used by the Bundler gem.

- **lib/:** Extended modules for your application.

- **log/:** Application log files.

- **package.json:** This file allows you to specify what npm dependencies are needed for your Rails application.

- **public/:** Contains static files and compiled assets. When your app is running, this directory will be exposed as-is.

- **Rakefile:** This file locates and loads tasks that can be run from the command line. The task definitions are defined throughout the components of Rails. Rather than changing Rakefile, you should add your own tasks by adding files to the lib/tasks directory of your application.

- **README.md:** This is a brief instruction manual for your application. You should edit this file to tell others what your application does, how to set it up, and so on.

- **storage/:** Active Storage files for Disk Service.

- **test/:** Unit tests, fixtures, and other test apparatus.

- **tmp/:** Temporary files (like cache and pid files).

- **vendor/:** A place for all third-party code. In a typical Rails application, this includes vendored gems.

- **.gitignore:** This file tells git which files (or patterns) it should ignore.

- **.ruby-version:** This file contains the default Ruby version.

By now you actually have a functional Rails application ready. To see it, you need to start a web server on your development machine by simply running the following command in the blog directory:

```
$ bin/rails server
```

And if you are using Windows, you have to insert the scripts under the bin folder directly to the Ruby interpreter via ruby bin\rails server.

This will start up Puma, a web server distributed with Rails by default. In order to see your application in action, you need to open a browser window and navigate to http://localhost:3000. You should see the Rails default information page saying: Yay! You're on Rails!

In case you want to stop the webserver, just press Ctrl+C in the terminal window where it is running. In the development environment, Rails does not generally require you to restart the server as any modifications you introduce in files will be automatically picked up by the server. Keep in mind that the "Yay! You're on Rails!" page is the smoke test for a new Rails application: it simply ensures that you have your software configured correctly enough to serve a page.

Saying "Hello" in Rails

To get Rails saying "Hello," one has to create at minimum a route, a controller with an action, and a view. It goes the following way: a route maps a request to a controller action, which then performs the necessary work to manage the request, and prepares any data for the view. A view then is expected to display data in the desired format.

In terms of correct execution: routes here stand for rules scripted in a Ruby Domain-Specific Language (DSL). Controllers are Ruby classes, and their public methods are actions. And views are templates, usually written in a combination of HTML and Ruby.

You start by adding a route to our routes file, config/routes.rb, at the top of the Rails.application.routes.draw block:

```
Rails.application.routes.draw do
  get "/articles", to: "articles#index"
end
```

This route basically declares that GET/articles requests are mapped to the index action of ArticlesController. And in order to create ArticlesController and its index action, you should run the controller generator using the --skip-routes option because we already have an appropriate route:

```
$ bin/rails generate controller Articles
index --skip-routes
```

With that, Rails will create the following files for you:[7]

- create app/controllers/articles_controller.rb

- invoke erb

- create app/views/articles

- create app/views/articles/index.html.erb

- invoke test_unit

- create test/controllers/articles_controller_test.rb

- invoke helper

- create app/helpers/articles_helper.rb

- invoke test_unit

- invoke assets

- invoke scss

- create app/assets/stylesheets/articles.scss

- create app/controllers/articles_controller.rb

- invoke erb

- create app/views/articles

- create app/views/articles/index.html.erb

- invoke test_unit

- create test/controllers/articles_controller_test.rb

- invoke helper
- create   app/helpers/articles_helper.rb
- invoke   test_unit
- invoke assets
- invoke   scss
- create   app/assets/stylesheets/articles.scss

The most essential of these is the controller file, app/controllers/articles_controller.rb. To illustrate with an example:

```
class ArticlesController <
ApplicationController
  def index
  end
end
```

As you can observe, the index action is empty. And when an action does not explicitly render a def index, Rails will automatically render an index that matches the name of the controller and action. Typically, the index action will render app/views/articles/index.html.erb by default. AS for now, let us open app/views/articles/index.html.erb, and replace its contents with:

```
<h1>Hello, Rails!</h1>
```

By default, the opening page displays "Yay! You're on Rails!" message. You change that and make it display "Hello, Rails!" text at http://localhost:3000. To achieve that, you can add a route that maps the root path of your application to the appropriate controller and action. Start by opening config/routes.rb, and inserting the following root route to the top of the Rails.application.routes.draw block:

```
Rails.application.routes.draw do
  root "articles#index"
  get "/articles", to: "articles#index"
end
```

With that you should be able to see the "Hello, Rails!" text when accessing the opening page, confirming that the root route is also mapped to the index action of ArticlesController.

MVC

By now we have discussed routes, controllers, actions, and views. All of these are key items of a web application that follows the MVC pattern. MVC is a design pattern that manages the responsibilities of an application to make it easier to reason about. Rails follows this design pattern in accordance with the convention principle.

But since we already have a controller and a view to work with, it is possible to generate the next essential piece: a model. A model stands for a Ruby class that is utilized to represent data. Additionally, models can communicate to the application's database through a feature of Rails called Active Record.

In order to define a model, you are expected to use the following model generator:

```
$ bin/rails generate model Article
title:string body:text
```

This will create the following files:[8]

- invoke active_record

- create db/migrate/<timestamp>_create_articles.rb

- create app/models/article.rb

- invoke test_unit

- create test/models/article_test.rb

- create test/fixtures/articles.yml

The two files that we shall use the most in the next Database Migrations section are the migration file (db/migrate/<timestamp>_create_articles.rb) and the model file (app/models/article.rb).

The last thing that is important to keep in mind while going along with this book is that model names are singular because an instantiated model represents a single data record. To help remember this principle, think of how you would call the model's constructor: you want to write Article.new(…), and not Articles.new(…).

DATABASE MIGRATIONS

Migrations are normally performed to advance the structure of an application's database. In Rails applications, migrations are scripted in Ruby so that they can be database-agnostic or enabled to work with various systems, rather than being customized for a single system.

---

[8] https://guides.rubyonrails.org/getting_started.html, Ruby on Rails

The content of a new migration file that we are going to establish here shall look the following way:

```
class CreateArticles <
ActiveRecord::Migration
  def change
    create_table :articles do |t|
      t.string :title
      t.text  :body
      t.timestamps
    end
  end
end
```

The above call to create_table states how the articles table should be constructed. By default, the create_table method adds an id column as an auto-incrementing primary standard. So the first record in the table will have an id of 1, the next record will have an id of 2, and so on.

Additionally, inside the block for create_table, you can observe two columns defined: title and body. These are typically inserted by the generator. On the last line of the block is a call to t.timestamps method that is used to define two additional columns named created_at and updated_at. There is no need to worry about these either as Rails will manage them for you, setting the values when you create or update a model object.

Now you can activate migration with the following command:

```
$ bin/rails db:migrate
```

This command is expected to display the output below indicating that the table was created:[9]

```
==   <CODE>CreateArticles: migrating ======
===============================
-- create_table(:articles)
   -> 0.0018s
==   CreateArticles: migrated (0.0018s)
==========================
```

Now you can interact with the table using this model. Moreover, you can apply the same model to manipulate the Database. But if you are going to do that, you would need to use a different feature of Rails called the console. The console stands for an interactive coding environment that automatically loads Rails with your application code. In order to launch the console, you need to insert the following command:

```
$ bin/rails console
```

Once activated, you should be able to see a prompt similar to this:

```
Loading development environment (Rails
6.0.2.1)
irb(main):001:0>
```

Using this prompt, you can initialize a new Article object:

```
irb> article = Article.new(title: "Hello
Rails", body: "I am on Rails!")
article = Article.new(title: "Hello Rails",
body: "I am on Rails!")
```

---

[9] https://guides.rubyonrails.org/getting_started.html, Ruby on Rails

It is important to understand that at this point you have only initialized this object. This object is not saved to the database just yet as it is only available in the console.

As an alternative, you can go back to the controller in app/controllers/articles_controller.rb, and change the index action to fetch all articles from the database:

```
class ArticlesController <
ApplicationController
  <CODE>def index
    @articles = Article.all
  end
end
```

The above controller instance variables can also be accessed by the view. That means you can reference @articles in app/views/articles/index.html.erb. To do that, you need to open the file, and replace its contents with:[10]

```
<h1>Articles</h1>
<ul>
  <% @articles.each do |article| %>
    <li>
      <%= article.title %>
    </li>
  <% end %>
</ul>
```

As you might notice, the above code is a mixture of HTML and ERB, a templating system that examines Ruby code embedded in a document. Here, we can see two types of

---

[10] https://guides.rubyonrails.org/getting_started.html, Ruby on Rails

ERB tags: <% %> and <%= %>. The <% %> tag means "check the enclosed Ruby code." The <%= %> tag means "check the enclosed Ruby code as well as the output value it returns." Anything you normally script in a regular Ruby program can go inside these ERB tags, though it is recommended to keep the contents of ERB tags short for better readability.

Since there is no need to output the value returned by @articles.each, we have enclosed that code in <% %>. But, since you need the output value returned by article.title (for each article), we have included that code in <%= %>.

It is possible to see the final result of all the modifications we have introduced in this chapter simply by visiting http://localhost:3000. And here is what would happen when you do that:

- The browser will send a request: GET http://localhost:3000.

- Your Rails application receives this request.

- The Rails router shall map the root route to the index action of ArticlesController.

- The index action will use the Article model to fetch all articles in the database.

- Rails will automatically render the app/views/articles/index.html.erb view.

- The ERB code in the view is examined to output HTML.

- The server shall send a response holding the HTML back to the browser.

And with that, you have connected all the Rails MVC components together and observed your first controller action.

In this chapter, you were introduced to the basic history and main features of Ruby on Rails. We also showed you how to install and configure essential features of the framework. You should now have the foundation required to be able to review and analyze Ruby on Rails syntax with its specific Terms, various Fields, Validations, and Files.

## CHAPTER 2

Getting Started with Ruby on Rails

IN THIS CHAPTER

➢ Getting to know the basic Ruby on Rails Syntax

➢ Configuring Ruby on Rails Fields and Validations

➢ Reviewing framework's generated files

In the previous chapter, we learned about the history of Ruby on Rails and its main characteristics and advantages. This chapter shall walk you through setting up your basic syntax and development environment so you can follow the instructions and examples in this book. First, we shall look at the structured form of the framework, review working with Fields and Validations, and learn more about its generated files.

DOI: 10.1201/9781003229605-2

BASIC RUBY ON RAILS SYNTAX

Ruby on Rails is a flexible and dynamic language. It is considered flexible mostly in terms of syntax. For instance, even if an object of a class is instantiated, you can still edit the method of the object. In addition, there is no need to specify the data type of variables. Once you move along with this book, you will learn about the syntax of Ruby in-depth and will see why it is so widely popular. In this chapter, we shall briefly go through the most important components of syntax.

Data Type

In ruby, there are three main types of data:

1. Number

2. String

3. Boolean

```
> number_of_student = 5 #number
 => 5
> name = "Jane" #String
 => "Jane"
```

```
> isFemale = true #boolean
=> true
```

Therefore, once you give any value to a variable, the variable will sort out data type depending on what value you gave. So there is no need to specify the data type as you might require in Java, for instance. As you observe here, once you give a number to a variable, its data type automatically becomes a number.

Naming Convention

1. Local variables, method parameters, and method names start with a lowercase letter or an underscore. To illustrate:

```
name, _28, fishAndChips
```

2. Global variable should start with $. For example:

```
$plan, $CUSTOMER
```

3. Instance variables are marked with @in the following way:

```
@name, @pw
```

4. Class variables start with @@ and must be initialized before using it:

```
@@plays, @@count
```

5. Class name or Constants start with an uppercase letter:

```
Person, PI
```

Input and Output

1. **puts:** used to print value and make new line

```
puts "Hello"
"Jane" => nil
```

2. **print:** applied to print value but does not make new line

```
print "Hello"
"James" #make new-line
⇨ nil
```

3. **gets:** used to get input from prompt

```
input = gets.chomp.to_i
chomp: Remove the portion corresponding
to this 'Enter'
to_i: convert input into integer value
```

Methods

1. **def:** a reserved word applied for declaring a method. To illustrate with an example:

```
def sum
  puts 2 + 2
end
sum or sum()
```

At the same time, if you like to make one method, you can use "def" keyword before the name of a method or make a block using the end keyword. In order to run the method, just call the name of a method or use parenthesis:

```
def sum(a,b)
  puts a + b
end
sum(4,5)
```

In case you need to give parameters on method, use parenthesis and put parameter variables. That way, when you call it, you would be calling method with parameters.

Class

- Typically starts with the "class" keyword

- The initialize method is used the same way as a constructor in Java

- Class variables begin with "@" are instance variables

The basic structure of Class follows a few certain rules:

- Variables starting with "@@" are treated as class variables that could be shared between objects of one class.

- At run-time, you can change the definition of a class, meaning that member variables/methods can be added/removed/redefined.

- In order to instantiate an object:

  - Without initializing, you can use "new" keyword— person = Person.new

- Call initialize with parameters if you have initialized method:

```
person = Person.new("adam",
"password")
```

Meantime, if you set out to write a Rails application, leaving aside the configuration and other rulebook chores, you
have to mainly focus on the following three tasks:

- **Describing and modeling your application's domain:**
  The domain is the central location of your application. The domain may be a music database, a phone
  book, an address book, or a software inventory. So
  here you have to decide what you want in it and what
  entities may exist in this universe, and how the components in it relate to each other. This could be viewed
  as equivalent to modeling a database structure to preserve all the entities and their relationship.

- **Specifying what happens in this domain:** The
  domain model is static, and it is up to you to make it
  dynamic. For instance, addresses can be added to an
  address book, song scores can be viewed from music
  stores, users can log in to a new dating app. You need
  to specify all the possible scenarios or actions that the
  components of your domain can participate in.

- **Choosing and designing the publicly available views
  of the domain:** At this point, you should be able to think
  about your domain in Web-browser terms. You can preview a welcome page, a registration page, or a confirmation page. Each of these pages, or views, demonstrates
  to the user how things are managed at a certain point.

Based on the above three tasks, Ruby on Rails deals with a Model/View/Controller (MVC) framework. The MVC principle divides the work of an application into three separate but closely cooperative subsystems that we have already briefly encountered in the previous chapter:

Model (ActiveRecord)

It regulates the relationship between the objects and the database and manages validation, association, and transactions. This subsystem is executed in the ActiveRecord library, which provides an interface and binding between the tables in a relational database and the Ruby program code that operates database records. Typically, Rails method names are automatically generated from the field names of database tables.

View (ActionView)

ActionView stands for a data illustration in a particular format, activated by a controller's decision to present the data. They are script-based template models similar to PHP that are quite easy to integrate with AJAX technology. This subsystem is executed in the ActionView library, which is an Embedded Ruby-based system for defining presentation templates for data presentation. Every Web connection to a Rails application eventually ends up in the displaying of a view.

Controller (ActionController)

ActionController stands for a facility within the application that regulates traffic, on the one hand, querying the models for specific data, and on the other hand, operating that data (searching, sorting, messaging it) into a form that satisfies the needs of a given view.

Assuming a directory representation of MVC framework with a default installation over Linux, you can find them like this:

```
tp> cd /usr/local/lib/ruby/gems/2.2.0/gems
tp> ls
```

With that, you will be able to see subdirectories including (but not limited to) the following:

```
actionpack-x.y.z
ActiveRecord-x.y.z
rails-x.y.z
```

Over a windows installation, you can find them like this:

```
tp>cd ruby\lib\ruby\gems\2.2.0\gems
ruby\lib\ruby\gems\2.2.0\gems\>dir
```

Most of the development work will be creating and editing files in the library/app subdirectories. Here is a brief overview of how to use them:

- The controller's subdirectory is where Rails looks to find controller classes. A controller manages a web request from the user.

- The views subdirectory contains the display templates to fill in with data from your application, convert to HTML, and return to the browser.

- The model's subdirectory contains the classes that shape the data stored in the application's database. In most frameworks, this section of the application can be quite messy and error-prone, but Rails keeps it very straightforward.

- The helper's subdirectory keeps any helper classes used to assist the MVC classes. This helps to keep the MVC code-focused, uncluttered, and short.

ADDING FIELDS

Fields in web applications are key features for user input. Nevertheless, fields markup can easily become tedious to fill and maintain because of the need to regulate field naming and other multiple attributes. Rails does it through view helpers for generating fields and forms markup. However, since these helpers have different use cases, it is important to know the differences between the helper methods before utilizing them.

The main field and form helper is form_with:

```
<%= form_with do |form| %>
  Form contents
<% end %>
```

When called without arguments like this, it creates a form tag which, when submitted, will POST to the current page. For instance, assuming the current page is a home page, the generated HTML will look like this:

```
<form accept-charset="UTF-8" action="/"
method="post">
  <input name="authenticity_token"
type="hidden" value="J7CBxfHalt49OSHp27hbl
qK20c9PgwJ108nDHX/8Cts=" />
  Form contents
</form>
```

You should be able to notice that the HTML has an input element with type hidden. This input is important here as non-GET forms cannot be successfully submitted without it. The hidden input component with the name authenticity_token is a security notion of Rails called cross-site request protection, and helpers generate it for every non-GET form (provided that this security feature is enabled).

Generic Search Form

Another basic form you see on the web is a search form. This form normally holds the following:

- a form element with "GET" method
- a label for the input
- a text input element
- a submit element

In order to create this form, you need to use form_with and the form builder object it yields:

```
<%= form_with url: "/search", method: :get
do |form| %>
  <%= form.label :query, "Search for:" %>
  <%= form.text_field :query %>
  <%= form.submit "Search" %>
<% end %>
```

This will generate the following HTML:

```
<form action="/search" method="get" accept-
charset="UTF-8" >
  <label for="query">Search for:</label>
```

```
  <input id="query" name="query"
type="text" />
  <input name="commit" type="submit"
value="Search" data-disable-with="Search" />
</form>
```

For every form input, an ID attribute is generated from its name. These IDs can be very helpful when it comes to CSS styling or manipulation of form controls with JavaScript. Additionally, you can use "GET" as the method for search forms. This allows users to bookmark a specific search and get back to it as well as use the right HTTP verb for an action.

Helpers for Generating Field and Form Elements

The form builder object form_with has various helper methods for generating fields and form elements such as text fields, checkboxes, and radio buttons. The first parameter to these methods is always the name of the input. When the form is submitted, the name will be forwarded along with the form data, and will make its way to the params in the controller with the value entered by the user for that field. For instance, if the form has <%= form.text_field :query %>, then you would be able to get the value of this field in the controller with params[:query].

When naming inputs, Rails uses specific conventions that make it possible to submit parameters with non-scalar values such as arrays or hashes, which will also be accessible in params. You can read more about them in chapter three of this book.

Checkboxes

Checkboxes are form controls that provide the user a set of options they can enable or disable:[1]

```
<%= form.check_box :pet_dog %>
<%= form.label :pet_dog, "I own a dog" %>
<%= form.check_box :pet_cat %>
<%= form.label :pet_cat, "I own a cat" %>
```

This generates the following:

```
<input type="checkbox" id="pet_dog"
name="pet_dog" value="1" />
<label for="pet_dog">I own a dog</label>
<input type="checkbox" id="pet_cat"
name="pet_cat" value="1" />
<label for="pet_cat">I own a cat</label>
```

The first parameter to check_box is the name of the input. The second parameter is the value of the input. When the checkbox is reviewed, this value will be included in the form data (and be present in params).

Radio Buttons

Radio buttons, while similar to checkboxes, are controls that identify a set of options in which they are mutually exclusive (meaning you can only pick one):

```
<%= form.radio_button :age, "child" %>
<%= form.label :age_child, "I am younger
than 18" %>
```

---

[1] https://guides.rubyonrails.org/form_helpers.html, Ruby on Rails

```
<%= form.radio_button :age, "adult" %>
<%= form.label :age_adult, "I am over 18" %>
```

```
Output:
<input type="radio" id="age_child"
name="age" value="child" />
<label for="age_child">I am younger than
18</label>
<input type="radio" id="age_adult"
name="age" value="adult" />
<label for="age_adult">I am over 18</label>
```

As with check_box, the second parameter to radio_button is the value of the input. Because these two radio buttons share the same name (age), the user will only be able to select one of them, and params[:age] will contain either "child" or "adult."

Another notable thing to mention would be to always use labels for checkbox and radio buttons. The link text with a specific option and, by expanding the clickable region, make it easier for users to find the inputs.

Other Helpers of Interest

Other form controls are text areas, hidden fields, password fields, number fields, date and time fields:[2]

```
<%= form.text_area :message, size: "70x5" %>
<%= form.hidden_field :parent_id, value:
"foo" %>
<%= form.password_field :password %>
<%= form.number_field :price, in:
1.0..20.0, step: 0.5 %>
```

---

[2] https://guides.rubyonrails.org/form_helpers.html, Ruby on Rails

```
<%= form.range_field :discount, in: 1..100 %>
<%= form.date_field :born_on %>
<%= form.time_field :started_at %>
<%= form.datetime_local_field :graduation_
day %>
<%= form.month_field :birthday_month %>
<%= form.week_field :birthday_week %>
<%= form.search_field :name %>
<%= form.email_field :address %>
<%= form.telephone_field :phone %>
<%= form.url_field :homepage %>
<%= form.color_field :favorite_color %>
```

The output would be:

```
<textarea name="message" id="message"
cols="70" rows="5">
<input type="hidden" name="parent_id"
id="parent_id" value="foo" />
<input type="password" name="password"
id="password" />
<input type="number" name="price" id="price"
step="0.5" min="1.0" max="20.0" />
<input type="range" name="discount"
id="discount" min="1" max="100" />
<input type="date" name="born_on" id="born_
on" />
<input type="time" name="started_at"
id="started_at" />
<input type="datetime-local"
name="graduation_day" id="graduation_day" />
<input type="month" name="birthday_month"
id="birthday_month" />
<input type="week" name="birthday_week"
id="birthday_week" />
```

```
<input type="search" name="name" id="name" />
<input type="email" name="address"
id="address" />
<input type="tel" name="phone" id="phone" />
<input type="url" name="homepage"
id="homepage" />
<input type="color" name="favorite_color"
id="favorite_color" value="#000000" />
```

Make sure to note that hidden inputs are not displayed to the user but instead hold data like any textual input. If necessary, values inside them can be changed with JavaScript.

The above-applied search, telephone, date, time, color, DateTime, DateTime-local, month, week, URL, email, number, and range inputs are HTML5 controls. In case you want your app to have a consistent experience in older browsers, you will need an HTML5 polyfill (code that implements a feature on web browsers that do not support a particular type of functionality). There are numerous solutions out there for this, although a popular service at the moment is Modernizr—https://modernizr.com/, which offers a simple way to add functionality based on the presence of detected HTML5 features.

Dealing with Model Objects

The :model argument of form_with allows us to connect the form builder object to a model object, meaning that the form will refer to that model object, and the form's fields will be populated with values from that model object. To illustrate, let us say we have an @article model object like:[3]

```
@article = Article.find(42)
# => #<Article id: 42, title: "My Title",
body: "My Body">
```

That is a part of the following form:

```
<%= form_with model: @article do |form| %>
  <%= form.text_field :title %>
  <%= form.text_area :body, size: "60x10" %>
  <%= form.submit %>
<% end %>
```

The output would then be:

```
<form action="/articles/42" method="post"
accept-charset="UTF-8" >
  <input name="authenticity_token"
type="hidden" value="..." />
  <input type="text" name="article[title]"
id="article_title" value="My Title" />
```

---

[3] https://guides.rubyonrails.org/form_helpers.html, Ruby on Rails

```
  <textarea name="article[body]"
id="article_body" cols="60" rows="10">
    My Body
  </textarea>
  <input type="submit" name="commit"
value="Update Article" data-disable-
with="Update Article">
</form>
```

A few things worth noticing here:

- The form action is automatically packed with an appropriate value for @article.

- The form fields are automatically filled with the corresponding values from @article.

- The form field names are connected to article[...] meaning that params[:article] will be a hash holding all these field's values.

- The submit button is automatically assigned an appropriate text value.

You should expect that your input will automatically mirror model attributes. However, If there is other information, you can include it in your form just as with attributes and access it via params[:article][:my_nifty_non_attribute_input].

The fields_for Helper

It is also possible to create a similar binding without actually creating <form> tags with the fields_for helper. This is most useful for editing additional model objects with the same form. For instance, if you had a Person model with an associated ContactDetail model, you could create a form for creating both like so:

```
<%= form_with model: @person do |person_
form| %>
  <%= person_form.text_field :name %>
  <%= fields_for :contact_detail, @person.
contact_detail do |contact_detail_form| %>
    <%= contact_detail_form.text_field
:phone_number %>
  <% end %>
<% end %>
```

Which would consequently produce the following output:

```
<form action="/people" accept-
charset="UTF-8" method="post">
  <input type="hidden" name="authenticity_
token" value="bL13x72p1dyDD8bgtkjKQakJCp
d4A8JdXGbfksxBDHdf1uC0kCMqe2tvVdUYfidJt0
fj3ihC4NxiVHv8GVYxJA==" />
  <input type="text" name="person[name]"
id="person_name" />
  <input type="text" name="contact_
detail[phone_number]" id="contact_detail_
phone_number" />
</form>
```

The object provided by fields_for is a form builder like the one offered by form_with.

ADDING VALIDATIONS

Validations are applied to ensure that only necessary data is saved into your database. For example, it may be important to your application to secure that every user inserts a valid email address and mailing address. Model-level validations would be the best way, in this case, to ensure that only valid data is saved into your database. They are database agnostic, cannot be bypassed by end-users, and are simple to test and maintain. Anyway, Rails provides additional built-in helpers for common needs and lets you create your own validation methods if needed.

There are several ways to validate data before it is saved into your database, including native database constraints, client-side validations, and controller-level validations. To summarize the main pros and cons:

- Database constraints and stored methods make the validation mechanisms database-dependent and can affect testing and maintenance making it more time-consuming. However, if your database is used by other applications, it may be better to use some constraints at the database level. Moreover, database-level validations can safely manage some processes such as going through heavily-used tables that could be difficult to run otherwise.

- Client-side validations are also very useful, but get generally unreliable if used alone. If they are executed using JavaScript, they may be omitted if JavaScript is turned off in the user's browser. However, if combined with other techniques, client-side validation can be the easiest way to provide users with immediate feedback as they browse your site.

   Controller-level validations can be tempting to apply, but they tend to become heavy and complex to test or maintain. Therefore, it is advised to know your controllers, as it will make your application a pleasure to operate within the long run. Another important thing is to choose controllers in regards to certain, specific cases and assignments.

Validations are typically activated when you create a fresh object that does not belong to the database yet using the new method. Once you call save upon that object, it will be saved into the appropriate database table. Active Record uses the new_record? instance method to decide whether an object is already in the database or not. Examine the following Active Record class:

```
class Person < ApplicationRecord
end
```

You can see how it works only by looking at the following bin/rails console output:

```
irb> p = Person.new(name: "John Doe")
=> #<Person id: nil, name: "John Doe",
created_at: nil, updated_at: nil>

irb> p.new_record?
=> true

irb> p.save
=> true

irb> p.new_record?
=> false
```

Setting a new record will send an SQL INSERT command to the database. Updating an existing record will send an

SQL UPDATE command instead. Validations are normally executed before these commands are forwarded to the database. If any validations fail, the object will be disregarded as invalid and Active Record will not permit the INSERT or UPDATE operation. This helps to prevent storing an invalid object in the database.

At the same time, there are many ways to change the state of an object in the database. Some methods might activate validations, but some will not. This means that it is possible to save an object in the database in an invalid state if you are not careful enough. The following methods activate validations, and will save the object to the database only if the object is valid:

```
create
create!
save
save!
update
update!
```

The bang versions raise an exception if the record is invalid and the non-bang versions do not.

The simples validation example looks the following way:

```
class Person < ApplicationRecord
  validates :name, presence: true
end

irb> Person.create(name: "Jane Austin").
valid?
=> true
irb> Person.create(name: nil).valid?
=> false
```

As you can observe, the above validation lets us know that the sample Person is not valid without a name attribute, therefore it will not be persisted in the database.

Skipping Validations

The following is the list of methods that skip validations, and are used to save the object to the database regardless of its validity. They should be used with caution:[4]

```
decrement!
decrement_counter
increment!
increment_counter
insert
insert!
insert_all
insert_all!
toggle!
touch
touch_all
update_all
update_attribute
update_column
update_columns
update_counters
upsert
upsert_all
```

Before saving an Active Record object, Rails examines your validations. In case these validations produce any errors,

---

[4] https://guides.rubyonrails.org/active_record_validations.html, Ruby on Rails

Rails does not proceed to saving the object. You can also run these validations on your own, use valid? to activate your validations and it shall return true if no errors were found in the object, and false otherwise. To demonstrate with an example:

```
class Person < ApplicationRecord
  validates :name, presence: true
end
irb> Person.create(name: "Jane Austin").
valid?
=> true
irb> Person.create(name: nil).valid?
=> false
```

After Active Record has completed checking validations, any errors found can be reviewed through the errors instance method, which returns a collection of errors. By definition, an object is valid if this collection is empty after running validations.

At the same time, keep in mind that an object instantiated with a new method will not report errors even if it is technically invalid, since validations are automatically run only when the object is saved, such as with the create or save methods:[5]

```
class Person < ApplicationRecord
  validates :name, presence: true
end
```

---

[5] https://guides.rubyonrails.org/active_record_validations.html, Ruby on Rails

```
Copy
irb> p = Person.new
=> #<Person id: nil, name: nil>
irb> p.errors.size
=> 0

irb> p.valid?
=> false
irb> p.errors.objects.first.full_message
=> "Name can't be blank"

irb> p = Person.create
=> #<Person id: nil, name: nil>
irb> p.errors.objects.first.full_message
=> "Name can't be blank"

irb> p.save
=> false

irb> p.save!
ActiveRecord::RecordInvalid: Validation
failed: Name can't be blank

irb> Person.create!
ActiveRecord::RecordInvalid: Validation
failed: Name can't be blank
```

Here, invalid? is the inverse of valid?, it activates your validations, returning true if any errors were found in the object, and false otherwise.

In order to confirm whether or not a particular attribute of an object is valid, you can use errors[:attribute]. It is supposed to return an array of all the error messages for :attribute, but if there are no errors on the specified attribute, an empty array is displayed. This method is only useful after validations have been executed because it only examines the errors collection and does not trigger validations itself. It is different from the invalid? method explained above since it does not particularly verify the validity of the object as a whole but only focuses to see whether there are errors found on an individual attribute of the object:

```
class Person < ApplicationRecord
  validates :name, presence: true
end
```

```
Copy
irb> Person.new.errors[:name].any?
=> false
irb> Person.create.errors[:name].any?
=> true
```

Validation Helpers

Rails has many pre-defined validation helpers that you can apply directly inside your class definitions. These helpers follow common validation rules and each time a validation fails, an error is added to the object's errors collection, associated with the attribute being validated.

Each helper accepts an arbitrary number of attribute names, so with a single line of code, you can include the same kind of validation to several attributes. At the same time, all of them accept the :on and :message options, which determine when the validation should be run and what message should be inserted to the errors collection if it fails. The :on option takes one of the values :create or :update. There is a default error message for each one of the validation helpers that is typically used when the :message option is not specified. In this section, we shall take a look at each one of the available helpers.

acceptance

This helper validates that a checkbox on the user interface was examined when a form was submitted. This is normally used when the user has to agree to your application's terms of service, confirm that some text is read, or any similar concept:

```
class Person < ApplicationRecord
  validates :terms_of_service, acceptance:
true
end
```

This check is completed only if terms_of_service is not nil. The default error message for this helper is "must be accepted" which can also pass as a custom message via the message option:

```
class Person < ApplicationRecord
  validates :terms_of_service, acceptance:
{ message: 'must be accepted' }
end
```

It is also possible to use an :accept option, which determines the allowed values that will be considered as accepted. It normally defaults to ["1", true] and can be easily modified:

```
class Person < ApplicationRecord
  validates :terms_of_service, acceptance:
{ accept: 'yes' }
```

```
  validates :eula, acceptance: { accept:
['TRUE', 'accepted'] }
end
```

However, this particular validation is very specific to web applications, and this "acceptance" does not need to be registered anywhere in your database. If you do not have a field for it, the helper will create a virtual component. If the field does exist in your database, the accept option should be set to true, or else the validation will not run.

validates_associated

This helper should be applied when your model has associations with other models, and they also need to be validated. When you save your object, valid? will be called upon each one of the associated objects in:

```
class Library < ApplicationRecord
  has_many :books
  validates_associated :books
end
```

This validation will operate on all of the association types. Yet you cannot use validates_associated on both ends of your associations as they would call each other in an infinite loop. The default error message for validates_associated is "is invalid" but each associated object will eventually hold its own errors collection.

confirmation

You can use this helper when you have two text fields that should receive exactly the same content. For instance, you may want to verify an email address or a password. This validation results in a virtual attribute with the name of the field that has to be confirmed with "_confirmation" appended:

```
class Person < ApplicationRecord
  validates :email, confirmation: true
end
```

As your view template you could use the following:

```
<%= text_field :person, :email %>
<%= text_field :person, :email_confirmation
%>
```

This check would be fully completed only if email_confirmation is not nil. To require confirmation, make sure to include a presence check for the confirmation attribute as follows:

```
class Person < ApplicationRecord
  validates :email, confirmation: true
  validates :email_confirmation, presence:
true
end
```

Alternatively, there is also a :case_sensitive option that you can apply to see whether the confirmation constraint will be case sensitive or not:

```
class Person < ApplicationRecord
  validates :email, confirmation: { case_
sensitive: false }
end
```

Keep in mind that the default error message for this helper would be—"does not match confirmation."

exclusion

This helper is used to validate that the attributes' values are not added in a given set, and set can be any enumerable object:

```
class Account < ApplicationRecord
  validates :subdomain, exclusion: { in:
%w(www us ca jp),
    message: "%{value} is reserved." }
end
```

As one can see, the exclusion helper has an option :in that holds the set of values that should not be accepted for the validated attributes. The :in option also has an alias called :within that you can apply for the similar purpose. The above example uses the :message option to illustrate how you can add the attribute's value.

format

This helper validates the attributes' values by checking whether they match a given regular statement, which is marked with the :with option:

```
class Product < ApplicationRecord
  validates :legacy_code, format: { with:
/\A[a-zA-Z]+\z/,
    message: "only allows letters" }
end
```

Alternatively, you might require that the specified component does not match the regular expression by using the

:without option. Keep in mind that the standard error message would be "is invalid."

inclusion

This helper sees that the attributes' values are included in a given set, where set can be any enumerable object:

```
class Coffee < ApplicationRecord
  validates :size, inclusion: { in:
%w(small medium large),
    message: "%{value} is not a valid size" }
end
```

This inclusion helper uses an option :in that holds the set of values that will be accepted. The :in option has an alternative called :within that you can utilize for the similar purpose. The default error message for this helper would be "is not included in the list."

length

This helper is applied to examine the length of the attributes' values. It has a variety of options, so you can define length constraints in various ways:[6]

```
class Person < ApplicationRecord
  validates :name, length: { minimum: 2 }
  validates :bio, length: { maximum: 500 }
  validates :password, length: { in: 6..20 }
  validates :registration_number, length:
{ is: 6 }
end
```

---

[6] https://guides.rubyonrails.org/active_record_validations.html, Ruby on Rails

The available length constraint options are:

- **:minimum:** The attribute shall not have less than the specified length.

- **:maximum:** The attribute shall not have more than the specified length.

- **:in (or :within):** The attribute length has to be included in a given interval. The value for this option must be a range.

- **:is:** The attribute length should be equal to the given value.

The default error messages in this case typically depend on the type of length validation being verified. It is possible to customize these messages using the :wrong_length, :too_long, and :too_short options and %{count} as a placeholder for the number corresponding to the length constraint being used:

```
class Person < ApplicationRecord
  validates :bio, length: { maximum: 1000,
    too_long: "%{count} characters is the
maximum allowed" }
end
```

Here, the default error messages would be plural, stating that it "is too short (minimum is %{count} characters)." For this reason, when :minimum is 1 it is recommended to provide a custom message or use presence: true instead. When :in or :within have a lower index of 1, you should either provide a custom message or call presence prior to length.

numericality

This helper makes sure that your attributes have only numeric values. By default, it will offer an optional sign followed by an integral or floating-point number.

In order to specify that only integral numbers are allowed, set :only_integer to true. Then it will activate the /\A[+-]?\d+\z/ regular expression to validate the attribute's value. Otherwise, it will attempt to convert the value to a number using Float. Floats here are cast to BigDecimal using the column's precision value or 15. To illustrate this helper with an example:

```
class Player < ApplicationRecord
  validates :points, numericality: true
  validates :games_played, numericality:
{ only_integer: true }
end
```

The default error message for :only_integer would be "must be an integer." However, besides :only_integer, this helper also accepts the following features to add constraints to acceptable values:

- **:greater_than:** States that the value must be greater than the supplied value. The default error message for this option is "must be greater than %{count}."

- **:greater_than_or_equal_to:** Indicates that the value must be greater than or equal to the supplied value. The default error message for this option is "must be greater than or equal to %{count}."

- **:equal_to:** Makes sure the value is equal to the supplied value. The default error message for this option is "must be equal to %{count}."

- **:less_than:** States that the value must be less than the supplied value. The default error message for this option is "must be less than %{count}."

- **:less_than_or_equal_to:** Indicates that the value must be less than or equal to the supplied value. The default error message for this option is "must be less than or equal to %{count}."

- **:other_than:** Marks that the value must be other than the supplied value. The default error message for this option is "must be other than %{count}."

- **:odd:** Sets out that the value has to be an odd number if set to true. The default error message for this option is "must be odd."

- **:even:** Makes sure the value is an even number if set to true. The default error message for this option is "must be even."

By default, numericality does not permit any nil values. You can use allow_nil: true option to enable it if absolutely necessary. The default error message when no options are identified is "is not a number."

presence
This helper ensures that the specified attributes are not empty. It applies the blank? method to see if the value is either nil or a blank string, that is either empty or has whitespace:

```
class Person < ApplicationRecord
  validates :name, :login, :email,
presence: true
end
```

In case you want to be sure that an association is present, you should test whether the associated object itself is present, and not the foreign key utilized to map the association. This way, it is not only examined that the foreign key is not empty but also that the referenced object is there:

```
class Supplier < ApplicationRecord
  has_one :account
  validates :account, presence: true
end
```

In order to review any associated records whose presence is required, you must include the :inverse_of option for the association:

```
class Order < ApplicationRecord
  has_many :line_items, inverse_of: :order
end
```

If you validate the presence of an object associated via a has_one or has_many relationship, it will see that the object is neither blank? nor marked_for_destruction?.

In case if false.blank? is true, you want to validate the presence of a boolean field using one of the following validations:

```
validates :boolean_field_name, inclusion:
[true, false]
validates :boolean_field_name, exclusion:
[nil]
```

By using one of these validations, you are making sure the value will NOT be nil which would result in a NULL value in most cases.

absence

This helper validates that the marked attributes are absent. It utilizes the present? method to check if the value is not either nil or a blank string:

```
class Person < ApplicationRecord
  validates :name, :login, :email, absence:
true
end
```

If you need to be certain about an association being absent, you will need to test whether the associated object itself is absent, and not the foreign key used to map the association:

```
class LineItem < ApplicationRecord
  belongs_to :order
  validates :order, absence: true
end
```

In order to review associated records whose absence is required, you should add the :inverse_of option to the association:

```
class Order < ApplicationRecord
  has_many :line_items, inverse_of: :order
end
```

Once you validate the absence of an object associated via a has_one or has_many relationship, it will check that the object is neither present? nor marked_for_destruction?.

uniqueness

This helper sees that the attribute's value is unique right before the object gets saved. It does not result in a uniqueness constraint in the database, so it may so occur that two different database connections produce two records with the same value for a column that you plan to make unique. To prevent that, it is advised to create a unique index on that column in your database:

```
class Account < ApplicationRecord
  validates :email, uniqueness: true
end
```

The validation processes by performing an SQL query into the model's table, looking for an existing record with the same value in that attribute. Additionally, there is a :scope option that you can apply to specify one or more components that are used to limit the uniqueness check:

```
class Holiday < ApplicationRecord
  validates :name, uniqueness: { scope:
:year,
    message: "should happen once per year"
}
end
```

In case you need to create a database constraint to avoid any violations of a uniqueness validation using the :scope option, you must do so by creating a unique index on both columns in your database. Moreover, there is also a :case_ sensitive option that you can add to determine whether the uniqueness constraint will be case sensitive or not:

```
class Person < ApplicationRecord
  validates :name, uniqueness: { case_
sensitive: false }
end
```

Keep in mind that some databases are specifically configured to perform case-insensitive searches anyway. The default error message for this validation is "has already been taken."

validates_with
This helper is used to forward the record to a separate class for validation:[7]

```ruby
class GoodnessValidator <
ActiveModel::Validator
  def validate(record)
    if record.first_name == "Evil"
      record.errors.add :base, "This person
is evil"
    end
  end
end
class Person < ApplicationRecord
  validates_with GoodnessValidator
end
```

Errors added to the above record.errors[:base] relate to the state of the record as a whole, and not to a certain attribute. In the meantime, the validates_with helper takes a class, or a list of classes to use for validation. Also worth noting that there is no default error message for validates_with since you are expected to manually add errors to the record's errors collection in the validator class.

---

[7] https://guides.rubyonrails.org/active_record_validations.html, Ruby on Rails

In order to implement the validate method, you must have a record parameter set and validated. Like all other validations, validates_with takes the :if, :unless and :on options. If you add any other options, it will forward those options to the validator class as options:

```
class GoodnessValidator <
ActiveModel::Validator
  def validate(record)
    if options[:fields].any? { |field|
record.send(field) == "Evil" }
      record.errors.add :base, "This person
is evil"
    end
  end
end
class Person < ApplicationRecord
  validates_with GoodnessValidator, fields:
[:first_name, :last_name]
end
```

The above-scripted validator will be initialized only once for the whole application life cycle, and not on each validation run, so you want to be thoughtful about inserting instance variables in it. If your validator is way too complicated that you want instance variables, you can easily use a basic Ruby object instead:

```
class Person < ApplicationRecord
  validate do |person|
    GoodnessValidator.new(person).validate
  end
end
```

```
class GoodnessValidator
  def initialize(person)
    @person = person
  end

  def validate
    if
some_complex_condition_involving_ivars_
and_private_methods?
      @person.errors.add :base, "This
person is evil"
    end
  end

  # ...
end
```

validates_each

This helper is applied to validate attributes against a block. It does not have a predefined validation function therefore you should create one using a block for each attribute to be passed to validates_each and be tested against it. To demonstrate with an example:

```
class Person < ApplicationRecord
  validates_each :name, :surname do
|record, attr, value|
    record.errors.add(attr, 'must start with
upper case') if value =~ /\A[[:lower:]]/
  end
end
```

As you can observe, the block receives the record, the attribute's name, and the attribute's value. With that, you can do anything you like to check for valid data within the block. In case your validation fails, you can include an error in the model, thus making it invalid.

Common Validation Options

Now let us review some common validation options:

allow_nil

The :allow_nil option disregards the validation when the value being validated is nil:

```
class Coffee < ApplicationRecord
  validates :size, inclusion: { in:
%w(small medium large),
    message: "%{value} is not a valid size"
}, allow_nil: true
end
```

allow_blank

The :allow_blank option is almost the same as the :allow_nil option. This option will permit validation pass if the attribute's value is blank?, like nil or an empty string for example:

```
class Topic < ApplicationRecord
  validates :title, length: { is: 5 },
allow_blank: true
end

irb> Topic.create(title: "").valid?
=> true
irb> Topic.create(title: nil).valid?
=> true
```

message

The :message option enables you to specify the message that will be included to the errors collection when validation fails. If this option is not used, Active Record activates the respective default error message for each validation helper. The :message option accepts both the String or Proc:

The String :message value can optionally hold any/all of %{value}, %{attribute}, and %{model} which will be automatically replaced when validation fails. This replacement is performed using the I18n gem, and the placeholders should match values exactly without leaving any spaces.

The Proc :message value is given two arguments :the object that is being validated, and a hash with :model, :attribute, and :value key-value pairs:

```
class Person < ApplicationRecord
  # Hard-coded message
  validates :name, presence: { message:
"must be given please" }
  # Message with dynamic attribute value.
%{value} will be replaced
  # with the actual value of the attribute.
%{attribute} and %{model}
  # are also available.
  validates :age, numericality: { message:
"%{value} seems wrong" }
  # Proc
  validates :username,
    uniqueness: {
      # object = person object being
validated
      # data = { model: "Person",
attribute: "Username", value: <username> }
```

```
      message: ->(object, data) do
         "Hey #{object.name},
#{data[:value]} is already taken."
      end
     }
end
```

on

The :on option lets you set when the validation should take place. The default trend for all the built-in validation helpers is to be executed on save (both when you are creating a new record and when you are updating it). If you want to modify it, you can use on: :create to run the validation only when a new record is created or on: :update to run the validation only when a record is updated. To illustrate with an example:

```
class Person < ApplicationRecord
  # it will be possible to update email
with a duplicated value
  validates :email, uniqueness: true, on:
:create

  # it will be possible to create the
record with a non-numerical age
  validates :age, numerically: true, on:
:update

  # the default (validates on both create
and update)
  validates :name, presence: true
end
```

You can also apply on :to determine custom contexts. Custom contexts need to be executed precisely by passing the name of the context to valid?, invalid?, or save:[8]

```
class Person < ApplicationRecord
  validates :email, uniqueness: true, on:
:account_setup
  validates :age, numericality: true, on:
:account_setup
end
```

```
irb> person = Person.new(age:
'thirty-three')
irb> person.valid?
=> true
irb> person.valid?(:account_setup)
=> false
irb> person.errors.messages
=> {:email=>["has already been taken"],
:age=>["is not a number"]}
```

```
person.valid?(:account_setup) executes
both the validations without saving the
model. person.save(context: :account_setup)
validates person in the account_setup
context before saving.
```

---

[8] https://guides.rubyonrails.org/active_record_validations.html, Ruby on Rails

When triggered by an explicit context, validations extent to that context as well:

```
class Person < ApplicationRecord
  validates :email, uniqueness: true, on:
:account_setup
  validates :age, numericality: true, on:
:account_setup
  validates :name, presence: true
end
```

```
Copy
irb> person = Person.new
irb> person.valid?(:account_setup)
=> false
irb> person.errors.messages
=> {:email=>["has already been taken"],
:age=>["is not a number"], :name=>["can't
be blank"]}
```

Strict Validations

It is also possible to specify validations to be strict and utilize ActiveModel::StrictValidationFailed when the object is invalid:

```
class Person < ApplicationRecord
  validates :name, presence: { strict:
true }
end
```

```
irb> Person.new.valid?
ActiveModel::StrictValidationFailed: Name
can't be blank
```

Additionally, there is also an option to pass a custom exception to the :strict option:

```
class Person < ApplicationRecord
  validates :token, presence: true,
uniqueness: true, strict:
TokenGenerationException
end

irb> Person.new.valid?
TokenGenerationException: Token can't be
blank
```

Conditional Validation

Depending on the project, it is typically advised to validate an object only when a given predicate is satisfied. You can do that by applying the :if and :unless options, which stands as a symbol, a Proc or an Array. You may also use the :if option when you need to mark when the validation should happen. If you need to specify when the validation should not happen, then you may use the :unless option.

Moreover, it is possible to associate the :if and :unless options with a symbol corresponding to the name of a method that will get called right before validation happens. This is the most commonly applied option:

```
class Order < ApplicationRecord
  validates :card_number, presence: true,
if: :paid_with_card?
  def paid_with_card?
    payment_type == "card"
  end
end
```

Using a Proc with :if and :unless

Similar to the above example, you can associate :if and :unless with a Proc object which will be called. Using a Proc object gives you a chance to write an inline condition instead of a separate method. This option is best suited for one-liners:

```
class Account < ApplicationRecord
  validates :password, confirmation: true,
    unless: Proc.new { |a| a.password.
blank? }
end
```

And since Lambdas are a type of Proc, they can also be applied to write inline conditions in a shorter way:

```
validates :password, confirmation: true,
unless: -> { password.blank? }
```

Grouping Conditional Validations

At some point you would want to have multiple validations use a singular condition. It can be easily done using with_ options validation:

```
class User < ApplicationRecord
  with_options if: :is_admin? do |admin|
    admin.validates :password, length: {
minimum: 10 }
    admin.validates :email, presence: true
  end
end
```

Make sure to note that all validations inside of the with_ options block will have automatically passed the condition if: :is_admin?

Combining Validation Conditions

On the other hand, if multiple conditions determine whether or not a validation should happen, an Array could be used. Moreover, you can apply both :if and :unless to the same validation:

```ruby
class Computer < ApplicationRecord
  validates :mouse, presence: true,
                    if: [Proc.new { |c|
c.market.retail? }, :desktop?],
                    unless: Proc.new { |c|
c.trackpad.present? }
end
```

Nevertheless, the validation only runs when all the :if conditions and none of them :unless conditions are evaluated to true.

At the same time, if you find that the built-in validation helpers are not enough for your needs, you can script your own validators or validation methods as you wish. Custom validators should be viewed as classes that inherit from ActiveModel::Validator. These classes must execute the validate method which takes a record as an argument and completes the validation on it. The custom validator is called using the validates_with method:[9]

```ruby
class MyValidator < ActiveModel::Validator
  def validate(record)
    unless record.name.start_with? 'X'
```

---

[9] https://guides.rubyonrails.org/active_record_validations.html, Ruby on Rails

```
        record.errors.add :name, "Need a
name starting with X please!"
    end
  end
end

class Person
  include ActiveModel::Validations
  validates_with MyValidator
end
```

The simplest way to add custom validators for vali-
dating individual components is with the convenient
ActiveModel::EachValidator. In this case, the custom
validator class must run a validate_each method which
includes three arguments: record, attribute, and value.
These correspond to the instance, the attribute to be validated, and the value of the attribute in the passed instance:

```
class EmailValidator <
ActiveModel::EachValidator
  def validate_each(record, attribute, value)
    unless value =~ /\A([^@\s]+)@
((?:[-a-z0-9]+\.)+[a-z]{2,})\z/i
      record.errors.add attribute,
(options[:message] || "is not an email")
    end
  end
end

class Person < ApplicationRecord
  validates :email, presence: true, email:
true
end
```

As shown in the example above, you can also mix standard validations with your own custom validators.

GENERATED FILES

Ruby on Rails is a full-fledged web framework that makes getting started with development easy due to its set of default files and folders. We have already provided a brief overview of this topic in chapter one, but this section explains the basic files and folders generated by Rails in detail.

- **app:** This is should be counted as the core directory of your entire app and most of the application-specific code is placed into this directory. Rails is an MVC framework, which means the application is separated into parts per its purpose in the MVC. And all three sections go inside this directory.

  - **app/assets:** This folder holds the static files necessary for the application's front-end set into folders based on their type. The javascript files and stylesheets (CSS) in these folders should be application-specific since the external library files would go into another directory.

  - **app/assets/images:** All the images planned for the application should locate in this directory. The images here are available in views through the Rails helpers like image_tag so that you do not have to specify the relative or absolute path for images.

  - **app/assets/javascripts:** The javascript files go into this directory. It is a common practice to create JS files for each controller. For instance, for books_controller.rb, the JS functions for this controller's views would be books.js.

- **app/assets/javascripts/application.js:** The precreated application.js is one of the statements for the entire application's javascript requirements. Rails use the asset pipeline for connecting and serving up assets. This means the application.js is the file where you reference the application-specific JS files, which are associated and minified before passing it to the views.

- **app/assets/stylesheets:** Similar to/javascript, the CSS files are located here. The naming convention is also the same as the javascript assets.

- **app/assets/stylesheets/application.css:** This file is a manifest for the stylesheets in your application. Similar to application.js, the referenced files are illustrated as a single stylesheet to the view.

- **app/controllers:** This is where all the controller files are located. Controllers are responsible for regulating the model and views. The script to generate a controller is:

```
rails generate controller controller_
name action1 action2
app/controllers/application_controller.
rb
```

This is the main controller from which all other controllers inherit. The methods on ApplicationController are available to other controllers as well. This controller inherits from the ActionController::Base module, which has a standard set of methods to operate controllers.

- **app/controllers/concerns:** Concerns are sets that can be applied across controllers. It is recommended to DRY your code by executing reusable functionality inside the directory. The original naming convention for this file is module_name.rb.

- **app/helpers:** This is where all the helper functions for views reside. There are already a few pre-created helpers available, like the one we reference above (image_tag) for referring to images in views. You can create your own functions in a controller-specific helper file, which will be automatically created when you use Rails generators to create the controller. The naming convention is controller_name_helper.rb.

  - **app/helpers/application_helper.rb:** This file is the default root helper. Similar to application_controller.rb, functions scripted here will be accessible by all the helpers and all the views.

- **app/mailers:** The mailers directory holds the mail-specific features for the application. Mailers are similar to controllers, and they will have their view files in app/views/mailer_name/. The first time you activate a mailer, application_mailer.rb is automatically generated for you. This will inherit from the ActionMailer::Base and sets the default from address and the layout for your mailer views; subsequent mailers will inherit from ApplicationMailer.

  The naming convention for this file is similar to controllers: modelname_mailer.rb.

- **app/models:** All model files are located in the app/ models directory. Models could be viewed as object-relational mappers to the database tables that contain the data. The naming convention is simply model-name.rb. The model name would be the singular form of the underlying table that represents the model in the database. For instance, the Book model will be mapped on top of the books table in the database.

  - **app/models/concerns:** Model concerns are similar to Controller concerns, holding methods that might be applied in multiple model files. This particular feature can greatly help when organizing the code.

- **app/views:** Views constitute an essential part of the MVC architecture. All the files related to the views go into this directory. The files are a combination of HTML and Ruby organized evenly based on the controller to which they correspond. Namely, there is a view file for each controller action.

  - **app/views/books/index.html.erb:** One of the Rails' conventions could be broken. Meaning that, if necessary, you can explicitly render any view manually.

  - **app/views/layouts:** This folder has the layout for all your view files that they inherit. Files placed here are available across all the view files.

    In addition, it is possible to create multiple layouts scoped to parts of the application. For instance, if you need to create a separate layout for administrative or user views, you can achieve it by creating a layout named after the controller name. For all AdminController views, it is better to create a layout file called admin.html.erb which will then act as the layout for the admin views, as well as any controller that inherits from AdminController. You can also generate partial views here that could be applied across multiple controllers.

- **app/views/layouts/application.html.erb:** This is the default file created automatically, which acts as the layout for actions in ApplicationController and any other controllers that inherit from ApplicationController.

- **bin:** This directory holds Binstubs for the Rails application. Binstubs here stand for wrappers that run gem executables modified for your application. The default available Binstubs are bundle, rails, rake, setup, and spring. Any of these binstubs can be activated by: bin/<executable>

- **config:** To put it simply, config files contain all the application's configuration files. The database connection and application behavior can be manipulated by the files inside this directory.

  - **config/application.rb:** This holds the main configuration for the application, such as the timezone, language, and many other settings. Any configurations made here automatically apply to all environments (development, test, and production).

Various environment-specific configurations will go into other files that we shall see below.

- **config/boot.rb:** boot.rb, as the name suggests, "boots" up the Rails application. Typically, Rails apps organize gem dependencies in a file called Gemfile in the root of the project. The Gemfile is the one holding all the dependencies necessary for the application to run. boot.rb makes sure that there is actually a Gemfile present and will store the path to this file in an environment variable called BUNDLE_GEMFILE for later use. However, boot.rb requires 'bundler/setup' which will build and regulate the gems located in the Gemfile using Bundler.

- **config/database.yml:** This file has all the database configuration the application needs. Here, various configurations could be set for different environments.

- **config/environment.rb:** This file contains application.rb necessary to initialize the Rails application.

- **config/routes.rb:** This is the routes file where your application could be defined.

- **config/secrets.yml:** This is a special place for you to store application secrets. The secrets defined could easily be accessed throughout the application via Rails.application.secrets.<secret_name>.

- **config/environments:** As stated before, this folder has the environment-specific configuration files

for the development, test, and production environments. Configurations in application.rb are
available in all environments. At the same time,
you can separate out complex configurations for
the different environments by adding settings to
the environment named files inside this directory. Default environment files available are—
development.rb, production.rb, test.rb, but it is
possible to add others as well if needed.

• **config/initializers:** This directory holds the list
of files that need to be run during the Rails initialization phase. Any *.rb file you create here
will run during the initialization automatically.
For instance, constants that you generate here
will then be available throughout your app. The
initializer file is activated from the call in config/
environment.rb to Rails.application.initialize.

There are a few core initializers, which we shall
go through below, but it is also possible for you
to add any Ruby file you like. As a matter of fact,
many Rails gems require an initializer to complete the setup of that gem for your Rails app.

• **config/initializers/assets.rb:** This holds all configurations for the asset pipeline. It will have
only one default configuration already predefined, Rails.application.config.assets.version,
which is the setting for your assets bundle. You
can then specify other configurations simply by
adding additional assets paths or other items to
precompile.

- **config/initializers/backtrace_silencers.rb:** Here you can add backtrace_silencers and various filters that are applicable for your app. Backtrace filters stand for filters that help to refine the notifications when an error occurs. Silencers, on the other hand, allow you to silence all the notifications from specified gems.

- **config/initializers/cookie_serializer.rb:** Not much configuration takes place in this file. It mainly contains specifications for the app's cookie serialization.

- **config/initializers/filter_parameter_logging.rb:** This file is specified for you to add parameters that might contain sensitive information and that you do not want otherwise displayed in your logs. By default, the "password" parameter is filtered in advance.

- **config/initializers/inflections.rb:** You can access this file in order to add or override the inflections (singularizations and pluralizations) for any language of your preference.

- **config/initializers/mime_type.rb:** This file was designed for you to add MIME (Multi-purpose Internet Mail Extensions) configurations for your application to manage different types of files you may need to use.

- **config/initializers/session_store.rb:** This file could be viewed as the underlying session platform for your app to save sessions. The default is :Cookie_store, meaning sessions are located in browser cookies, but you can change it to :CacheStore (to store the data in the Rails cache), :ActiveRecordStore (stores the data in a database using Active Record) or :MemCacheStore (stores the data in a memcached cluster).

- **config/initializers/wrap_parameters.rb:** As the name suggests, it holds settings for wrapping your parameters. By default, all the parameters are combined into a nested hash so that it is available without a root.

- **config/locales:** This has the list of YAML files (data serialization language that is utilized for writing configuration files) for each language with the keys and values to translate certain app components.

- **db:** All the database-related files could be found in this folder. The configuration, schema, and migration files can be accessed here, along with various seed files.

  - **db/seeds.rb:** This file is used to prefill or regulate databases with specific pre-requisite records. In case you are looking for methods for record insertion, you can use the standard ActiveRecord.

- **Gemfile:** As previously mentioned, the Gemfile is the place where all your app's gem dependencies are generated. This file is mandatory, as it includes the Rails core gems, among other gems.

- **Gemfile.lock:** Gemfile.lock contains the gem dependency tree, including all versions of the app. This file is generated by bundle install of the above Gemfile. It, in effect, locks your app dependencies to specific versions.

- **lib:** To put it simply, the lib directory is where all the application-specific libraries locate. Application-specific libraries stand for re-usable generic code extracted from the application. You may as well think of it as an application-specific gem.

  - **lib/assets:** This file contains all the library assets, as well as several items that are not application-specific, like scripts, stylesheets, and images.

  - **lib/tasks:** The application's ongoing tasks and can be reviewed through this directory.

With that, we have come to the conclusion of this chapter. Understanding the directory and file structure of a Rails application can take you a long way to mastering Rails. Please take time to go through the information and sample code referenced here as it will help you on your journey to becoming a full-fledged Rails developer. In the next chapter, we shall focus on Ruby Data Types, such as String, Numbers, Arrays, Hashes, and Symbols.

## CHAPTER 3

Ruby Data Types

IN THIS CHAPTER

➤ Learning about Ruby Object Oriented Functionalities

➤ Defining essential Ruby Data types

➤ Reviewing Data types' built-in methods

Ruby is a fundamentally object-oriented language, and everything appears to Ruby as an object. Every value in Ruby comes through as an object, including the most basic components: strings, numbers, and true/false features. Even a class itself becomes an object that is an instance of the Class class. This chapter will take you through all the major data types functionalities related to object-oriented Ruby.

To start with, one has to understand that a class in Ruby is used to identify the form of an object and to combine data representation and methods for manipulating that data into one neat set. The data and methods within a class

DOI: 10.1201/9781003229605-3

are called members of the class. Once you define a class, you determine a blueprint for a data type. This does not particularly define any data, but it does define what the class name would be, that is, what an object of the class will consist of and what operations can be executed on such an object.

A class definition has to start with the keyword class followed by the class name and is delimited with an end. For example, let us define the Box class using the keyword class as follows:

```
class Box
    code
end
```

Here, the name must begin with a capital letter, and by convention, names that have more than one word are run together with each word capitalized and no separating characters.

Typically, when you start learning a programming language, you should start by learning about its data types, variables, operators, conditionals, looping, and then into more various principles. In this chapter, we will see what is Ruby on Rails data type and how we can define it in different ways.

Ruby has several data types and all ruby data types are based on classes. The following are the basic data types recognized in Ruby:

- String

- Numbers

- Arrays and Hashes

- Symbols

These items cover more than 90% of all built-in data types that you will be using on a day-to-day basis working with Ruby.

Numbers and Strings (which is just another name for "texts") are some of the most basic data types that you deal with in Ruby on a regular basis. They could also be viewed as lego bricks that you need to master handling in order to get access to more interesting features, such as how objects, classes, and methods relate to each other.

Symbols are also very commonly used, a special kind of concept. You normally would not need to understand Symbols in order to script your own code. Nevertheless, we are still going to cover them briefly and use them once in a while.

Arrays and Hashes are objects that are applied to store other programming features, and they are very useful and widely popular. We shall see why later on.

STRING

A String object in Ruby operates and regulates an arbitrary order of one or more bytes, typically representing characters that mimic human language.

The simplest string literals are enclosed in single quotes (with the apostrophe character). The text within the quote marks is the literal value of the string:

'This is a basic Ruby string literal'

In case you want to place an apostrophe within a single-quoted string literal, precede it with a backslash so that the Ruby interpreter does not regard it as a termination of the string:

```
'Won\'t you read O\'Reilly\'s article?'
```

The backslash could also be applied to escape another backslash so that the second backslash is not itself interpreted as an escape character.

Following are the standard string-related features of Ruby:

Expression Substitution

Expression substitution is an instrument of inserting the value of any Ruby expression into a string using # { and }:[1]

```
#!/usr/bin/ruby

x, y, z = 12, 36, 72
puts "The value of x is #{ x }."
puts "The sum of x and y is #{ x + y }."
puts "The average was #{ (x + y + z)/3 }."
This will produce the following result -

The value of x is 12.
The sum of x and y is 48.
The average was 40.
```

General Delimited Strings

Using general delimited strings, you can create strings inside a pair of matching though arbitrary delimiter characters like, !, (, {, <, preceded by a percent character (%). General delimited strings examples:

```
%{Ruby is great.}  equivalent to " Ruby is
great."
%Q{ Ruby is great. } equivalent to " Ruby
is great. "
```

---

[1] https://www.tutorialspoint.com/ruby/ruby_strings.htm, Tutorialspoint

```
%q[Ruby is great.]  equivalent to a single-
quoted string
%x!ls! equivalent to backtick command
output 'ls'
```

Escape Characters

It is important to remember when dealing with escape characters that in a double-quoted string, an escape character is interpreted, but in a single-quoted string, an escape character is preserved. Following is a list of escape or nonprintable characters that can be represented with the backslash notation:[2]

Backslash notation	Hexadecimal character	Description
\a	0x07	Bell or alert
\b	0x08	Backspace
\cx		Control-x
\C-x		Control-x
\e	0x1b	Escape
\f	0x0c	Form feed
\M-\C-x		Meta-Control-x
\n	0x0a	Newline
\nnn		Octal notation
\r	0x0d	Carriage return
\s	0x20	Space
\t	0x09	Tab
\v	0x0b	Vertical tab
\x		Character x
\xnn		Hexadecimal notation

---

[2] https://docs.ruby-lang.org/en/2.4.0/syntax/literals_rdoc.html, Ruby

Character Encoding

The default character set for Ruby is ASCII, whose characters are represented by single bytes. If you use UTF-8-character encoding or another character set, items may be represented in one to four bytes.

At the same time, it is possible to change your character set using $KCODE at the beginning of your program, similar to—$KCODE = 'u'. Following are the possible values for $KCODE:

- a ASCII (same as none). This is the default.

- e- EUC.

- n- None (same as ASCII).

- u- UTF-8.

String Built-in Methods

It is required to have an instance of String object in order to call a String method. Following is the way to create an instance of String object:

```
new [String.new(str = "")]
```

This will return a new string object containing a copy of *str*. Now, using str object, you can use any available instance methods. For instance:

```
#!/usr/bin/ruby
myStr = String.new("THIS IS A SAMPLE")
foo = myStr.downcase
puts "#{foo}"
```

This will produce the following result:

```
this is a sample
```

Following Table 3.1 presents the public String methods (assuming str is a String object).

TABLE 3.1   List of Public String Methods[3]

1	**str % arg** Formats a string using a format specification. arg must be an array if it contains more than one substitution.
2	**str * integer** Returns a new string containing integer times str. In other words, str is repeated integer times.
3	**str + other_str** Concatenates other_str to str.
4	**str << obj** Concatenates an object to str. If the object is a Fixnum in the range 0.255, it is converted to a character.
5	**str <=> other_str** Compares str with other_str, returning -1 (less than), 0 (equal), or 1 (greater than). The comparison is case-sensitive.
6	**str == obj** Tests str and obj for equality. If obj is not a String, returns false; returns true if str <=> obj returns 0.
7	**str =~ obj** Matches str against a regular expression pattern obj. Returns the position where the match starts; otherwise, false.
8	**str.capitalize** Capitalizes a string.
9	**str.capitalize!** Same as capitalize, but changes are made in place.

(Continued)

---

[3] https://www.tutorialspoint.com/ruby/ruby_strings.htm, Tutorialspoint

TABLE 3.1   *(Continued)* List of Public String Methods

10	**str.casecmp**
	Makes a case-insensitive comparison of strings.
11	**str.center**
	Centers a string.
12	**str.chomp**
	Removes the record separator ($/), usually \n, from the end of a string. If no record separator exists, does nothing.
13	**str.chomp!**
	Same as chomp, but changes are made in place.
14	**str.chop**
	Removes the last character in str.
15	**str.chop!**
	Same as chop, but changes are made in place.
16	**str.concat(other_str)**
	Concatenates other_str to str.
17	**str.count(str, ...)**
	Counts one or more sets of characters. If there is more than one set of characters, counts the intersection of those sets
18	**str.crypt(other_str)**
	Applies a one-way cryptographic hash to str. The argument is the salt string, which should be two characters long, each character in the range a.z, A.Z, 0.9,. or /.
19	**str.delete(other_str, ...)**
	Returns a copy of str with all characters in the intersection of its arguments deleted.
20	**str.delete!(other_str, ...)**
	Same as delete, but changes are made in place.
21	**str.downcase**
	Returns a copy of str with all uppercase letters replaced with lowercase.
22	**str.downcase!**
	Same as downcase, but changes are made in place.
23	**str.dump**
	Returns a version of str with all nonprinting characters replaced by \nnn notation and all special characters escaped.

(Continued)

TABLE 3.1   *(Continued)* List of Public String Methods

24   **str.each(separator = $/) { |substr| block }**
Splits str using argument as the record separator ($/ by default),
passing each substring to the supplied block.

25   **str.each_byte { |fixnum| block }**
Passes each byte from str to the block, returning each byte as a
decimal representation of the byte.

26   **str.each_line(separator=$/) { |substr| block }**
Splits str using argument as the record separator ($/ by default),
passing each substring to the supplied block.

27   **str.empty?**
Returns true if str is empty (has a zero-length).

28   **str.eql?(other)**
Two strings are equal if they have the same length and content.

29   **str.gsub(pattern, replacement) [or]**
str.gsub(pattern) { |match| block }
Returns a copy of str with all occurrences of pattern replaced
with either replacement or the value of the block. The pattern
will typically be a Regexp; if it is a String then no regular
expression metacharacters will be interpreted (that is, /\d/ will
match a digit, but '\d' will match a backslash followed by a 'd')

30   **str[fixnum] [or] str[fixnum,fixnum] [or] str[range] [or]**
str[regexp] [or] str[regexp, fixnum] [or] str[other_str]
References str, using the following arguments: one Fixnum,
returns a character code at fixnum; two Fixnums, returns a
substring starting at an offset (first fixnum) to length (second
fixnum); range, returns a substring in the range; regexp
returns portion of matched string; regexp with fixnum,
returns matched data at fixnum; other_str returns substring
matching other_str. A negative Fixnum starts at end of string
with -1.

31   **str[fixnum] = fixnum [or] str[fixnum] = new_str [or]**
str[fixnum, fixnum] = new_str [or] str[range] = aString [or]
str[regexp] = new_str [or] str[regexp, fixnum] = new_str [or]
str[other_str] = new_str]
Replace (assign) all or part of a string.

(Continued)

TABLE 3.1 *(Continued)* List of Public String Methods

32	**str.gsub!(pattern, replacement) [or] str.gsub!(pattern) { |match|block }** Performs the substitutions of String#gsub in place, returning str, or nil if no substitutions were performed.
33	**str.hash** Returns a hash based on the string's length and content.
34	**str.hex** Treats leading characters from str as a string of hexadecimal digits (with an optional sign and an optional 0x) and returns the corresponding number. Zero is returned on error.
35	**str.include? other_str [or] str.include? fixnum** Returns true if str contains the given string or character.
36	**str.index(substring [, offset]) [or]** **str.index(fixnum [, offset]) [or]** **str.index(regexp [, offset])** Returns the index of the first occurrence of the given substring, character (fixnum), or pattern (regexp) in str. Returns nil if not found. If the second parameter is present, it specifies the position in the string to begin the search.
37	**str.insert(index, other_str)** Inserts other_str before the character at the given index, modifying str. Negative indices count from the end of the string, and insert after the given character. The intent is to insert a string so that it starts at the given index.
38	**str.inspect** Returns a printable version of str, with special characters escaped.
39	**str.intern [or] str.to_sym** Returns the Symbol corresponding to str, creating the symbol if it did not previously exist.
40	**str.length** Returns the length of str.
41	**str.ljust(integer, padstr = ' ')** If integer is greater than the length of str, returns a new String of length integer with str left-justified and padded with padstr; otherwise, returns str.

(Continued)

TABLE 3.1 *(Continued)* List of Public String Methods

| 42 | **str.lstrip** |
| | Returns a copy of str with leading whitespace removed. |

43 **str.lstrip!**
Removes leading whitespace from str, returning nil if no change
was made.

44 **str.match(pattern)**
Converts pattern to a Regexp (if it isn't already one), then invokes
its match method on str.

45 **str.oct**
Treats leading characters of str as a string of octal digits (with an
optional sign) and returns the corresponding number. Returns 0
if the conversion fails.

46 **str.replace(other_str)**
Replaces the contents and taintedness of str with the
corresponding values in other_str.

47 **str.reverse**
Returns a new string with the characters from str in reverse order.

48 **str.reverse!**
Reverses str in place.

49 **str.rindex(substring [, fixnum]) [or]**
str.rindex(fixnum [, fixnum]) [or]
str.rindex(regexp [, fixnum])
Returns the index of the last occurrence of the given substring,
character (fixnum), or pattern (regexp) in str. Returns nil if not
found. If the second parameter is present, it specifies the
position in the string to end the search.characters beyond this
point won't be considered.

50. **str.rjust(integer, padstr = ' ')**
If integer is greater than the length of str, returns a new String of
length integer with str right-justified and padded with padstr;
otherwise, returns str.

51 **str.rstrip**
Returns a copy of str with trailing whitespace removed.

52 **str.rstrip!**
Removes trailing whitespace from str, returning nil if no change
was made.

(Continued)

TABLE 3.1   *(Continued)* List of Public String Methods

53	**str.scan(pattern)** [**or**] **str.scan(pattern) { |match, ...| block }** Both forms iterate through str, matching the pattern (which may be a Regexp or a String). For each match, a result is generated and either added to the result array or passed to the block. If the pattern contains no groups, each individual result consists of the matched string, $&. If the pattern contains groups, each individual result is itself an array containing one entry per group.
54	**str.slice(fixnum)** [**or**] **str.slice(fixnum, fixnum)** [**or**] **str.slice(range)** [**or**] **str.slice(regexp)** [**or**] **str.slice(regexp, fixnum)** [**or**] **str.slice(other_str)** See str[fixnum], etc. **str.slice!(fixnum)** [**or**] **str.slice!(fixnum, fixnum)** [**or**] **str.slice!(range)** [**or**] **str.slice!(regexp)** [**or**] **str.slice!(other_str)** Deletes the specified portion from str, and returns the portion deleted. The forms that take a Fixnum will raise an IndexError if the value is out of range; the Range form will raise a RangeError, and the Regexp and String forms will silently ignore the assignment.
55	**str.split(pattern = $, [limit])** Divides str into substrings based on a delimiter, returning an array of these substrings. If the pattern is a String, then its contents are used as the delimiter when splitting str. If the pattern is a single space, str is split on whitespace, with leading whitespace and runs of contiguous whitespace characters ignored. If the pattern is a Regexp, str is divided where the pattern matches. Whenever the pattern matches a zero-length string, str is split into individual characters. If the pattern is omitted, the value of $; is used. If $; is nil (which is the default), str is split on whitespace as if ` ` were specified. If the limit parameter is omitted, trailing null fields are suppressed. If the limit is a positive number, at most that number of fields will be returned (if the limit is 1, the entire string is returned as the only entry in an array). If negative, there is no limit to the number of fields returned, and trailing null fields are not suppressed.

(Continued)

TABLE 3.1 *(Continued)* List of Public String Methods

56	**str.squeeze([other_str]*)**
	Builds a set of characters from the other_str parameter(s) using the procedure described for String#count. Returns a new string where runs of the same character that occur in this set are replaced by a single character. If no arguments are given, all runs of identical characters are replaced by a single character.
57	**str.squeeze!([other_str]*)**
	Squeezes str in place, returning either str or nil if no changes were made.
58	**str.strip**
	Returns a copy of str with leading and trailing whitespace removed.
59	**str.strip!**
	Removes leading and trailing whitespace from str. Returns nil if str was not altered.
60	**str.sub(pattern, replacement) [or]** **str.sub(pattern) { |match| block }**
	Returns a copy of str with the first occurrence of pattern replaced with either replacement or the value of the block. The pattern will typically be a Regexp; if it is a String, then no regular expression metacharacters will be interpreted.
61	**str.sub!(pattern, replacement) [or]** **str.sub!(pattern) { |match| block }**
	Performs the substitutions of String#sub in place, returning str, or nil if no substitutions were performed.
62	**str.succ [or] str.next**
	Returns the successor to str.
63	**str.succ! [or] str.next!**
	Equivalent to String#succ, but modifies the receiver in place.
64	**str.sum(n = 16)**
	Returns a basic n-bit checksum of the characters in str, where n is the optional Fixnum parameter, defaulting to 16. The result is simply the sum of the binary value of each character in str modulo 2n - 1.

(Continued)

TABLE 3.1 *(Continued)* List of Public String Methods

65	**str.swapcase**

Returns a copy of str with uppercase alphabetic characters
converted to lowercase and lowercase characters converted to
uppercase.

66 **str.swapcase!**

Equivalent to String#swapcase, but modifies the receiver in place,
returning str, or nil if no changes were made.

67 **str.to_f**

>Returns the result of interpreting leading characters in str as a
floating-point number. Extraneous characters past the end of a
valid number are ignored. If there is not a valid number at the
start of str, 0.0 is returned. This method never raises an
exception.

68 **str.to_i(base = 10)**

Returns the result of interpreting leading characters in str as an
integer base (base 2, 8, 10, or 16). Extraneous characters past the
end of a valid number are ignored. If there is not a valid number
at the start of str, 0 is returned. This method never raises an
exception.

69 **str.to_s [or] str.to_str**

Returns the receiver.

70 **str.tr(from_str, to_str)**

Returns a copy of str with the characters in from_str replaced by
the corresponding characters in to_str. If to_str is shorter than
from_str, it is padded with its last character. Both strings may
use the c1.c2 notation to denote ranges of characters, and
from_str may start with a ^, which denotes all characters except
those listed.

71 **str.tr!(from_str, to_str)**

Translates str in place, using the same rules as String#tr. Returns
str, or nil if no changes were made.

72 **str.tr_s(from_str, to_str)**

Processes a copy of str as described under String#tr, then
removes duplicate characters in regions that were affected by the
translation.

(Continued)

TABLE 3.1 *(Continued)* List of Public String Methods

73	**str.tr_s!(from_str, to_str)**
	Performs String#tr_s processing on str in place, returning str, or nil if no changes were made.
74	**str.unpack(format)**
	>Decodes str (which may contain binary data) according to the format string, returning an array of each value extracted. The format string consists of a sequence of single-character directives. Each directive may be followed by a number, indicating the number of times to repeat with this directive. An asterisk (*) will use up all remaining elements. The directives still may each be followed by an underscore (_) to use the underlying platform's native size for the specified type; otherwise, it uses a platform-independent consistent size. Spaces are ignored in the format string.
75	**str.upcase**
	Returns a copy of str with all lowercase letters replaced with their uppercase counterparts. The operation is locale insensitive. Only characters a to z are affected.
76	**str.upcase!**
	Changes the contents of str to uppercase, returning nil if no changes are made.
77	**str.upto(other_str) { |s| block }**
	Iterates through successive values, starting at strand ending at other_str inclusive, passing each value in turn to the block. The String#succ method is used to generate each value.

NUMBERS

A number in Ruby could be defined as a series of digits, utilizing a dot as a decimal mark. Additionally, the user can use the underscore as a separator. At the same time, there are different kinds of numbers like integers and float. An extended list of number types is presented in Table 3.2.[4]

---

[4] https://www.javatpoint.com/ruby-data-types, Javatpoint

TABLE 3.2   Types of Numbers

Class	Description	Example
Fixnum	They are normal numbers	1
Bignum	They are big numbers	111111111111
Float	Decimal numbers	3.0
Complex	Imaginary numbers	4 + 3i
Rational	They are fractional numbers	9/4
BigDecimal	Precision decimal numbers	6.0

Integers

Integers should be viewed as a subset of the real numbers. They are written without a fraction or a decimal component and fall within a set Z = {..., -2, -1, 0, 1, 2, ...}, therefore making this set absolutely infinite.

In computer languages, integers are standard data types. In practice, computers can only manage a subset of integer values, due to computers' having limited capacity. Integers are used to count discrete entities. Thus, we can have 3, 4 or 6 humans, but we cannot have 4.44 humans. Yet unlike in languages like Java or C, integers in Ruby are objects. Let us illustrate integers with the following example:

```
integers.rb
#!/usr/bin/ruby

p -2
p 121
p 123265
p -34253464356
p 34867367893463476

p 1.class
p 23453246.class
```

```
p 234532423563456346.class
p 234532423563232363463456456346.class

p 5 / 2
p 5.div 2
```

Make sure you notice that there could be positive and negative integer values of various sizes like in this piece of the above-mentioned code:

```
p -2
p 121
p 123265
p -34253464356
p 34867367893463476
```

This set is used to illustrate the class of integers:

```
p 1.class
p 23453246.class
p 234532423563456346.class
p 234532423563232363463456456346.class
```

Remaining two lines show integer division.

```
p 5 / 2
p 5.div 2
```

When we divide two integers using the integer division operator/method, the result is an integer as well:

```
$ ./integers.rb
-2
121
```

```
123265
-34253464356
34867367893463476
Integer
Integer
Integer
Integer
2
2
```

Integers can be specified in different notations in Ruby: decimal, hexadecimal, octal, and binary. Decimal numbers are used normally, as we know them. Hexadecimal numbers are preceded with 0x characters, octal with 0 character and binary with 0b characters. In this code example, let us print decimal 122 in various notation:

```
inotations.rb
#!/usr/bin/ruby

puts 122
puts 0x7a
puts 0172
puts 0b1111010
```

The output of the example would then be:

```
$ ./inotations.rb
122
122
122
122
```

When we work with integers, we operate with discrete items. To demonstrate, we could use integers to count books.

```
books.rb
#!/usr/bin/ruby

shelves = 16
books_on_shelves = 24

total = shelves * books_on_shelves

puts "There are total of #{total} books"
```

In this program, we count the total amount of books. Working with integers, the output of the program would be:

```
$ ./books.rb
There are total of 384 books
```

Big numbers might be difficult to read and get used to. If we have a number like 245342395423452, you will not be able to read it quickly. That is why outside computers, big numbers are separated by spaces or commas. For readability, Ruby allows integers to contain underscores. Yet underscores in integers are omitted by the Ruby interpreter. The example demonstrates the general use of underscores:

```
underscore.rb
#!/usr/bin/ruby

p 23482345629
p 23_482_345_629
p 23482345629 == 23_482_345_629
```

This line shows that the two numbers are actually equal:

```
p 23482345629 == 23_482_345_629
```

And the output would therefore be the following:

```
$ ./underscore.rb
23482345629
23482345629
True
```

Floating-Point Numbers

Floating-point numbers stand for real numbers of computing. And real numbers are mostly applied to measure continuous quantities like weight, height, or speed. In Ruby, decimal numbers are objects of the Float or a BigDecimal class. The BigDecimal class, a Ruby basic class, is part of Ruby's standard library.

One needs to know that decimal numbers cannot be precise, and all float objects represent only inexact real numbers. Let us illustrate floating-point values in the following example[5]:

```
decimals.rb
#!/usr/bin/ruby

p 15.4
p 0.3455
p -343.4563
```

---

[5] https://zetcode.com/lang/rubytutorial/datatypes/, Zetcode

```
p 12.5.class
p -12.5.class
p (5.0 / 2).class

p 5.fdiv 2
p 12.to_f
```

This part of the code represents three decimal numbers that have a decimal point character.p 15.4:

```
p 0.3455
p -343.4563
```

The following code lines show the types of numbers. All are floats and Integer division applied on the last one produces a Float too:

```
p 12.5.class
p -12.5.class
p (5.0 / 2).class
```

Here we produce floating-point values by applying the floating-point fdiv division method and the conversion to_f method:

```
p 5.fdiv 2
p 12.to_f
```

This would be the final output:

```
$ ./decimals.rb
15.4
0.3455
-343.4563
```

```
Float
Float
Float
2.5
12.0
```

By default, a decimal number is represented with a maximum 16 numbers after the decimal point. But it is also possible to control the format of floating-point values with the sprintf or printf methods. Basic formatting of decimal numbers could be completed in the following format:

```
format_float.rb
#!/usr/bin/ruby

p 1/3.0
p 1.fdiv 2

puts sprintf "%.4f" % (1/3.0)
puts sprintf "%.7f" % (5/3.0)
```

The first line shows a decimal with 16 places after the point. The second line prints two numbers after the point:

```
p 1/3.0
p 13.fdiv 4
p 1.fdiv 2
```

Here you can control the number of values after the decimal point using the sprintf method. There is a precision in the format specifier of the sprintf method. It is a number following the % character. The f is a conversion specifier that indicates you are dealing with floating-point values:

```
puts sprintf "%.4f" % (1/3.0)
puts sprintf "%.7f" % (5/3.0)
```

The output would be the following:

```
$ ./format_float.rb
0.3333333333333333
3.25
0.5
0.3333
1.6666667
```

Ruby also supports the use of scientific notation for floating-point values. Also known as exponential notation, it is a manner of including numbers too large or small to be conveniently scripted in standard decimal notation. This example shows two decimal numbers written in scientific notation:

```
scientific.rb
#!/usr/bin/ruby


p 1.2e-3
p 0.0012


p 1.5E-4
p 0.00015
```

The output of the above program would then be:

```
$ ./scientific.rb
0.0012
0.0012
0.00015
0.00015
```

As we have previously stated, floating-point values could be inaccurate. For most basic computations, ordinary floating-point numbers are sufficiently exact: considering that it might not be that important if you are dealing with the weight of 60 kg or 60.000019 kg. For other computations, including many scientific and engineering applications, precision is of utmost importance. That is why Ruby has a BigDecimal in the standard library. This particular class is used to provide arbitrary precision for very large or very accurate floating-point numbers. In this example, we compare the precision of a Float compared to a BigDecimal:[6]

```
big_decimal.rb
#!/usr/bin/ruby
require 'bigdecimal'
sum = 0

1000.times do
    sum = sum + 0.0001
end
p sum
```

---

[6] https://zetcode.com/lang/rubytutorial/datatypes/, Zetcode

```
sum = BigDecimal("0")
1000.times do
    sum = sum + BigDecimal("0.0001")
end

puts sum.to_s('F')
puts sum.to_s('E')
```

Keep in mind that the BigDecimal class should be imported:

```
require 'bigdecimal'
```

After that, you are expected to form a loop, where you add a small floating-point value to a sum variable. As a result, there will be a small inaccuracy:

```
sum = 0
1000.times do
    sum = sum + 0.0001
end
p sum
```

You can create the same loop with the BigDecimal values sum = BigDecimal("0"):

```
1000.times do
    sum = sum + BigDecimal("0.0001")
end
```

The sum would then be displayed in floating-point and engineering notation:

```
puts sum.to_s('F')
puts sum.to_s('E')
```

This output clearly shows how computing with BigDecimal is more precise than with Floats:

```
$. /big_decimal.rb
0.10000000000000184
0.1
0.1e0
```

Ruby Rational Numbers

Additionally, Ruby has built-in support for rational numbers as well. A rational number stands for an exact number. Using rational numbers, we avoid the chance to get rounding errors. In Ruby, a rational number is an object of the Rational class. Meaning that you can create rational numbers with a special to_r method from some objects.

A rational number is any number that can be evoked as a fraction of two integers a/b, where b!=0. Since b may be equal to 1, every integer is a rational number. This example illustrates a few rational numbers:

```
rationals.rb
#!/usr/bin/ruby

puts 2.to_r
puts "23".to_r
puts 2.6.to_r

p Rational 0
p Rational 1/5.0
p Rational 0.5
```

This line of code converts a 2 integer to 2/1 rational number using the to_r method:

```
puts 2.to_r
```

And here you create a rational number using the Rational class:

```
p Rational 0.5
```

The output of the above manipulation would then be:

```
$ ./rationals.rb
2/1
23/1
5854679515581645/2251799813685248
(0/1)
(3602879701896397/18014398509481984)
(1/2)
```

Ruby Nil Value

Ruby has a special value nil that represents an absolute absence of a value. The nil is a singleton object of a NilClass. There can only be one-nil, and thus you cannot have more of it. To demonstrate with an example:[7]

```
nil_value.rb
#!/usr/bin/ruby

puts nil
p nil
```

```
p $val
p [1, 2, 3][4]
p $val1 == $val2
```

Naturally, when you print the nil value to the console, the puts method prints an empty string while the p method prints 'nil' string:

```
puts nil
p nil
```

If you try to refer to a global variable that was not set, you will eventually get the nil value:

```
p $val
```

In the following line of code, if you refer to the fourth element of a three-element array, you will get nil. Because many methods in Ruby return nil for invalid values:

```
p [1, 2, 3][3]
```

At the same time, the next line shall return true. This is a consequence of the fact that the nil value is a singleton object of a NilClass:

```
p $val1 == $val2
$ ./nil_value.rb
nil
nil
nil
true
```

ARRAYS AND HASHES

Ruby arrays are ordered, an integer-indexed listing of objects. Each item in an array is linked with and referred to by an index.

Array indexing starts at 0, as in C or Java. A negative index is read relative to the end of the array—that is, an index of -1 indicates the last element of the array, -2 is the next to last element in the array, and so on.

Moreover, Ruby arrays can consist of objects such as String, Integer, Fixnum, Hash, Symbol, and even other Array objects. Ruby arrays are not as fixed as arrays in other languages; they tend to grow automatically while adding elements to them. There are many ways to create or initialize an array. One way is with the new class method:

```
names = Array.new
```

You can also edit the size of an array at the time of creating array:

```
names = Array.new(10)
```

Yet keep in mind that the array names have a size or length of 20 elements. But you can return the size of an array with either the size or length methods:

```
#!/usr/bin/ruby
names = Array.new(10)
puts names.size # This returns 10
puts names.length # This also returns 10
```

This will produce the following result:

```
10
10
```

It is also possible to assign a value to each element in the array as follows:

```
#!/usr/bin/ruby
names = Array.new(4, "book")
puts "#{names}"
```

This will produce the following result:

```
["book", " book ", " book ", " book "]
```

You can also apply a block through the new method, populating each element with what the block evaluates to:

```
#!/usr/bin/ruby
nums = Array.new(10) { |e| e = e * 2 }
puts "#{nums}"
```

This will produce the following output:

```
[0, 2, 4, 6, 8, 10, 12, 14, 16, 18]
```

One more form of array creation is as follows:

```
nums = Array[1, 2, 3, 4,5]
```

In addition, the Kernel module available in core Ruby has an Array method, which only accepts a single argument. This method takes a range as an argument to create an array of digits:

```
#!/usr/bin/ruby
digits = Array(0..9)
puts "#{digits}"
```

Which will produce the following result:

```
[0, 1, 2, 3, 4, 5, 6, 7, 8, 9]
```

Array Built-in Methods

It is required to have an instance of Array object to call an Array method. As we have already stated, the following is the way to create an instance of Array object:

```
Array (…) [or] Array[…] [or] […]
```

This will return a new array populated with the given objects. Now, using the created object, you can call any available instance methods. For instance:

```
#!/usr/bin/ruby
digits = Array(0..9)
num = digits.at(6)
puts "#{num}"
```

This will produce the following result:

It is also important to know the public array methods. Following is the table (Table 3.3) of the most widely-used public methods (assuming array is an array object)[8]:

TABLE 3.3   The Public Array Methods

1	**array & other_array** Returns a new array containing elements common to the two arrays, with no duplicates.
2	**array * int [or] array * str** Returns a new array built by concatenating the int copies of self.
3	**array + other_array** Returns a new array built by concatenating the two arrays together to produce a third array.
4	**array - other_array** Returns a new array that is a copy of the original array, removing any items that also appear in other_array.
5	**array <=> other_array** Compares str with other_str, returning -1 (less than), 0 (equal), or 1 (greater than). The comparison is case-sensitive.
6	**array | other_array** Returns a new array by joining array with other_array, removing duplicates.
7	**array << obj** Pushes the given object onto the end of array. This expression returns the array itself, so several appends may be chained together.
8	**array <=> other_array** Returns an integer (-1, 0, or +1) if this array is less than, equal to, or greater than other_array.
9	**array == other_array** Two arrays are equal if they contain the same number of elements and if each element is equal to (according to Object.==) the corresponding element in the other array.

(Continued)

---

[8] https://www.tutorialspoint.com/ruby/ruby_arrays.htm, Tutorialspoint

TABLE 3.3   *(Continued)* The Public Array Methods

10	**array[index] [or] array[start, length] [or]**
	array[range] [or] array.slice(index) [or]
	array.slice(start, length) [or] array.slice(range)
	Returns the element at index, or returns a subarray starting at start and continuing for length elements, or returns a subarray specified by range. Negative indices count backward from the end of the array (-1 is the last element). Returns nil if the index (or starting index) is out of range.
11	**array[index] = obj [or]**
	array[start, length] = obj or an_array or nil [or]
	array[range] = obj or an_array or nil
	Sets the element at index, or replaces a subarray starting at start and continuing for length elements, or replaces a subarray specified by range. If indices are greater than the current capacity of the array, the array grows automatically. Negative indices will count backward from the end of the array. Inserts elements if the length is zero. If nil is used in the second and third form, deletes elements from self.
12	**array.abbrev(pattern = nil)**
	Calculates the set of unambiguous abbreviations for the strings in *self*. If passed a pattern or a string, only the strings matching the pattern or starting with the string are considered.
13	**array.assoc(obj)**
	Searches through an array whose elements are also arrays comparing obj with the first element of each contained array using obj.==. Returns the first contained array that matches or *nil* if no match is found.
14	**array.at(index)**
	Returns the element at index. A negative index counts from the end of self. Returns nil if the index is out of range.
15	**array.clear**
	Removes all elements from array.
16	**array.collect { |item| block } [or]**
	array.map { |item| block }
	Invokes block once for each element of self. Creates a new array containing the values returned by the block.

(Continued)

TABLE 3.3   *(Continued)* The Public Array Methods

17   **array.collect! { |item| block } [or]**
      array.map! { |item| block }
      Invokes block once for each element of self, replacing the element
      with the value returned by block.

18   **array.compact**
      Returns a copy of self with all nil elements removed.

19   **array.compact!**
      Removes nil elements from array. Returns nil if no changes were
      made.

20   **array.concat(other_array)**
      Appends the elements in other_array to self.

21   **array.delete(obj) [or]**
      array.delete(obj) { block }
      Deletes items from self that are equal to obj. If the item is not
      found, returns nil. If the optional code block is given, it returns
      the result of the block if the item is not found.

22   **array.delete_at(index)**
      Deletes the element at the specified index, returning that
      element, or nil if the index is out of range.

23   **array.delete_if { |item| block }**
      Deletes every element of self for which block evaluates to
      true.

24   **array.each { |item| block }**
      Calls block once for each element in self, passing that element as
      a parameter.

25   **array.each_index { |index| block }**
      Same as Array#each, but passes the index of the element instead
      of the element itself.

26   **array.empty?**
      Returns true if the self array contains no elements.

27   **array.eql?(other)**
      Returns true if array and other are the same object, or are both
      arrays with the same content.

(Continued)

TABLE 3.3   *(Continued)* The Public Array Methods

28   **array.fetch(index) [or]**
array.fetch(index, default) [or]
array.fetch(index) { |index| block }
Tries to return the element at position index. If index lies outside
the array, the first form throws an IndexError exception, the
second form returns default, and the third form returns the
value of invoking block, passing in index. Negative values of
index count from the end of the array.

29   **array.fill(obj) [or]**
array.fill(obj, start [, length]) [or]
array.fill(obj, range) [or]
array.fill { |index| block } [or]
array.fill(start [, length]) { |index| block } [or]
array.fill(range) { |index| block }
The first three forms set the selected elements of self to obj. A
start of nil is equivalent to zero. A length of nil is equivalent to
self.length. The last three forms fill the array with the value of
the block. The block is passed with the absolute index of each
element to be filled.

30   **array.first [or]**
array.first(n)
Returns the first element, or the first n elements, of the array. If
the array is empty, the first form returns nil, and the second
form returns an empty array.

31   **array.flatten**
Returns a new array that is a one-dimensional flattening of this
array (recursively).

32   **array.flatten!**
Flattens array in place. Returns nil if no modifications were
made. (array contains no subarrays.)

33   **array.frozen?**
Returns true if array is frozen (or temporarily frozen while being
sorted).

34   **array.hash**
Computes a hash-code for array. Two arrays with the same
content will have the same hash code.

(Continued)

TABLE 3.3   *(Continued)* The Public Array Methods

---

35   **array.include?(obj)**
      Returns true if obj is present in self, false otherwise.

36   **array.index(obj)**
      Returns the index of the first object in self that is == to obj.
      Returns nil if no match is found.

37   **array.indexes(i1, i2, ... iN) [or]**
      array.indices(i1, i2, ... iN)
      This methods is deprecated in latest version of Ruby so please use
      Array#values_at.

38   **array.indices(i1, i2, ... iN) [or]**
      array.indexes(i1, i2, ... iN)
      This method is deprecated in the latest version of Ruby, so please
      use Array#values_at.

39   **array.insert(index, obj...)**
      Inserts the given values before the element with the given index
      (which may be negative).

40   **array.inspect**
      Creates a printable version of the array.

41   **array.join(sep = $,)**
      Returns a string created by converting each element of the array
      to a string, separated by sep.

42   **array.last [or] array.last(n)**
      Returns the last element(s) of self. If array is empty, the first form
      returns nil.

43   **array.length**
      Returns the number of elements in self. May be zero.

44   **array.map { |item| block } [or]**
      array.collect { |item| block }
      Invokes block once for each element of self. Creates a new array
      containing the values returned by the block.

45   **array.map! { |item| block } [or]**
      array.collect! { |item| block }
      Invokes block once for each element of array, replacing the
      element with the value returned by block.

(Continued)

TABLE 3.3 *(Continued)* The Public Array Methods

46 **array.items**
Returns the number of non-nil elements in self. May be zero.

47 **array.pack(aTemplateString)**
Packs the contents of the array into a binary sequence according to the directives in a TemplateString. Directives A, a, and Z may be followed by a count, which gives the width of the resulting field. The remaining directives also may take a count, indicating the number of array elements to convert. If the count is an asterisk (*), all remaining array elements will be converted. Any of the directives is still may be followed by an underscore (_) to use the underlying platform's native size for the specified type; otherwise, they use a platform-independent size. Spaces are ignored in the template string.

48 **array.pop**
Removes the last element from an array and returns it, or nil if array is empty.

49 **array.push(obj, ...)**
Pushes (appends) the given obj onto the end of this array. This expression returns the array itself, so several appends may be chained together.

50 **array.rassoc(key)**
Searches through the array whose elements are also arrays. Compares key with the second element of each contained array using ==. Returns the first contained array that matches.

51 **array.reject { |item| block }**
Returns a new array containing the items array for which the block is not true.

52 **array.reject! { |item| block }**
Deletes elements from array for which the block evaluates to true, but returns nil if no changes were made. Equivalent to Array#delete_if.

53 **array.replace(other_array)**
Replaces the contents of array with the contents of other_array, truncating or expanding if necessary.

(Continued)

TABLE 3.3 *(Continued)* The Public Array Methods

54	**array.reverse**
	Returns a new array containing array's elements in reverse order.
55	**array.reverse!**
	Reverses array in place.
56	**array.reverse_each {|item| block }**
	Same as Array#each, but traverses array in reverse order.
57	**array.rindex(obj)**
	Returns the index of the last object in array == to obj. Returns nil if no match is found.
58	**array.select {|item| block }**
	Invokes the block passing in successive elements from an array, returning an array containing those elements for which the block returns a true value.
59	**array.shift**
	Returns the first element of self and removes it (shifting all other elements down by one). Returns nil if the array is empty.
60	**array.size**
	Returns the length of array (number of elements).
61	**array.slice(index) [or] array.slice(start, length) [or] array.slice(range) [or] array[index] [or] array[start, length] [or] array[range]**
	Returns the element at index, or returns a subarray starting at start and continuing for length elements, or returns a subarray specified by range. Negative indices count backward from the end of the array (-1 is the last element). Returns nil if the index (or starting index) are out of range.
62	**array.slice!(index) [or] array.slice!(start, length) [or] array.slice!(range)**
	Deletes the element(s) given by an index (optionally with a length) or by a range. Returns the deleted object, subarray, or nil if the index is out of range.
63	**array.sort [or] array.sort { | a,b | block }**
	Returns a new array created by sorting self.
64	**array.sort! [or] array.sort! { | a,b | block }**
	Sorts self.

(Continued)

TABLE 3.3   *(Continued)* The Public Array Methods

65	**array.to_a** Returns self. If called on a subclass of Array, converts the receiver to an Array object.
66	**array.to_ary** Returns self.
67	**array.to_s** Returns self.join.
68	**array.transpose** Assumes that self is an array of arrays and transposes the rows and columns.
69	**array.uniq** Returns a new array by removing duplicate values in the array.
70	**array.uniq!** Removes duplicate elements from self. Returns nil if no changes are made (that is, no duplicates are found).
71	**array.unshift(obj, ...)** Prepends objects to the front of the array, other elements up one.
72	**array.values_at(selector,...)** Returns an array containing the elements in self corresponding to the given selector (one or more). The selectors may be either integer indices or ranges.
73	**array.zip(arg, ...) [or]** **array.zip(arg, ...){	arr	block }** Converts any arguments to arrays, then merges elements of the array with corresponding elements from each argument.

Hashes

A Hash is a set of key-value pairs like this: "job" = > "assignment." It is similar to an Array, but the indexing it uses is done via arbitrary keys of any object type, not an integer index.

The order in which you employ a hash by either key or value may seem arbitrary and will generally not be in the insertion feature. If you try to access a hash with a key that is not verified, the method will return nil.

As with arrays, there are many ways to create hashes. You can create an empty hash with the new class method:

```
months = Hash.new
```

Or you can use new to create a hash with a default value, which is otherwise just nil:

```
months = Hash.new( "month" )
or
months = Hash.new "month"
```

When you access any key in a hash that has a default value, if the key or value has not been identified, accessing the hash will return the default value:

```
#!/usr/bin/ruby
months = Hash.new( "month" )
puts "#{months[0]}"
puts "#{months[72]}"
```

This will return the following output:

```
month
month
```

Hash Built-in Methods

It is essential to have an instance of Hash object to call a Hash method. As we have illustrated before, the following is the way to create an instance of Hash object:

```
Hash[[key =>|, value]* ] or
Hash.new [or] Hash.new(obj) [or]
Hash.new { |hash, key| block }
```

This will return a new hash populated with the given objects. Now using the created object, you can call any available instance methods. To demonstrate with an example:

```
#!/usr/bin/ruby
$, = ", "
months = Hash.new( "month" )
months = {"1" => "January", "2" =>
"February"}
keys = months.keys
```

This will produce the following value:

```
["1", "2"]
```

Moreover, there are multiple public hash methods you may apply in your work[9] (Table 3.4).

TABLE 3.4   The Public Hash Methods

1	**hash == other_hash**
	Tests whether two hashes are equal, based on whether they have the same number of key-value pairs, and whether the key-value pairs match the corresponding pair in each hash.
2	**hash.[key]**
	Using a key, references a value from hash. If the key is not found, returns a default value.
3	**hash.[key] = value**
	Associates the value given by value with the key given by key.
4	**hash.clear**
	Removes all key-value pairs from hash.

(Continued)

---

[9] https://www.tutorialspoint.com/ruby/ruby_hashes.htm, Tutorialspoint

TABLE 3.4   *(Continued)* The Public Hash Methods

5	**hash.default(key = nil)** Returns the default value for hash, nil if not set by default=. ([] returns a default value if the key does not exist in hash.)
6	**hash.default = obj** Sets a default value for hash.
7	**hash.default_proc** Returns a block if hash was created by a block.
8	**hash.delete(key) [or]** **array.delete(key) { |key| block }** Deletes a key-value pair from hash by key. If block is used, returns the result of a block if pair is not found.
9	**hash.delete_if { |key,value| block }** Deletes a key-value pair from hash for every pair the block evaluates to true.
10	**hash.each { |key,value| block }** Iterates over hash, calling the block once for each key, passing the key-value as a two-element array.
11	**hash.each_key { |key| block }** Iterates over hash, calling the block once for each key, passing key as a parameter.
12	**hash.each_key { |key_value_array| block }** Iterates over hash, calling the block once for each key, passing the key and value as parameters.
13	**hash.each_key { |value| block }** Iterates over hash, calling the block once for each key, passing value as a parameter.
14	**hash.empty?** Tests whether hash is empty (contains no key-value pairs), returning true or false.
15	**hash.fetch(key [, default]) [or]** **hash.fetch(key) { | key | block }** Returns a value from hash for the given key. If the key can't be found, and there are no other arguments, it raises an IndexError exception; if default is given, it is returned; if the optional block is specified, its result is returned.

(Continued)

TABLE 3.4 *(Continued)* The Public Hash Methods

16	**hash.has_key?(key) [or] hash.include?(key) [or]** **hash.key?(key) [or] hash.member?(key)** Tests whether a given key is present in hash, returning true or false.
17	**hash.has_value?(value)** Tests whether hash contains the given value.
18	**hash.index(value)** Returns the key for the given value in hash, nil if no matching value is found.
19	**hash.indexes(keys)** Returns a new array consisting of values for the given key(s). Will insert the default value for keys that are not found.
20	**hash.indices(keys)** Returns a new array consisting of values for the given key(s). Will insert the default value for keys that are not found.
21	**hash.inspect** Returns a pretty print string version of hash.
22	**hash.invert** Creates a new hash, inverting keys and values from hash; that is, in the new hash, the keys from hash become values and values become keys.
23	**hash.keys** Creates a new array with keys from hash.
24	**hash.length** Returns the size or length of hash as an integer.
25	**hash.merge(other_hash) [or]** **hash.merge(other_hash) { |key, oldval, newval| block }** Returns a new hash containing the contents of hash and other_hash, overwriting pairs in hash with duplicate keys with those from other_hash.
26	**hash.merge!(other_hash) [or]** **hash.merge!(other_hash) { |key, oldval, newval| block }** Same as merge, but changes are done in place.
27	**hash.rehash** Rebuilds hash based on the current values for each key. If values have changed since they were inserted, this method reindexes hash.

(Continued)

TABLE 3.4   *(Continued)* The Public Hash Methods

28	**hash.reject { |key, value| block }** Creates a new hash for every pair the block evaluates to true
29	**hash.reject! { |key, value| block }** Same as reject, but changes are made in place.
30	**hash.replace(other_hash)** Replaces the contents of hash with the contents of other_hash.
31	**hash.select { |key, value| block }** Returns a new array consisting of key-value pairs from hash for which the block returns true.
32	**hash.shift** Removes a key-value pair from hash, returning it as a two-element array.
33	**hash.size** Returns the size or length of hash as an integer.
34	**hash.sort** Converts hash to a two-dimensional array containing arrays of key-value pairs, then sorts it as an array.
35	**hash.store(key, value)** Stores a key-value pair in hash.
36	**hash.to_a** Creates a two-dimensional array from hash. Each key/value pair is converted to an array, and all these arrays are stored in a containing array.
37	**hash.to_hash** Returns hash (self).
38	**hash.to_s** Converts hash to an array, then converts that array to a string.
39	**hash.update(other_hash) [or]** **hash.update(other_hash) {|key, oldval, newval| block}** Returns a new hash containing the contents of hash and other_hash, overwriting pairs in hash with duplicate keys with those from other_hash.
40	**hash.value?(value)** Tests whether hash contains the given value.

(Continued)

TABLE 3.4 *(Continued)* The Public Hash Methods

41	**hash.values**
	Returns a new array containing all the values of hash.
42	**hash.values_at(obj, ...)**
	Returns a new array containing the values from hash that is associated with the given key or keys.

SYMBOLS

Symbols are an interesting concept, and we need to introduce them because they are used so often and widely that you will very likely find them used in Ruby code as well. A symbol is written like this: :symbol. Meaning that there is a word that is preceded by a colon. This means that normally symbols do not contain spaces. Instead, if you have symbols that consist of multiple words you would have to concatenate them with underscores, like so: :another_key_symbol

You might also wonder, when to use strings, and when to use symbols? Unfortunately, there is actually no perfectly clear line or simple definition. One simple rule to follow would be that if the text at hand is handled as "data," then use a string. If it is code, then use a symbol, especially when applied as keys in hashes.

Another way of looking at symbols is that they are not really text, even though they are quite readable. Instead, they are unique identifiers, like numbers, or bar codes. While strings represent data that can change, symbols represent unique values, which are fixed.

To be more specific, if you use strings that hold the same text in your code multiple times, then a new string object will be created every time. For instance, if you put "Hello!" 10 times, then 10 actual string objects will be created (and later discarded, because they are not being used any longer). On the other hand, if you would apply a symbol for this and put :hello 10 times, then only one single object will be created and re-used.

A Symbol must be viewed as one of the most basic Ruby objects you can create that has a name and an internal ID. Symbols are useful because a given symbol name refers to the same object throughout a Ruby program. At the same time, Symbols are more efficient than strings. Two strings with the same contents are perceived as two different objects, but for any given name, there is only one Symbol object. This can save both time and memory, referring to the following example: p039symbol.rb:[10]

```
# p039symbol.rb
# use the object_id method of class Object
# it returns an integer identifier for an
object
puts "string".object_id
puts "string".object_id
puts :symbol.object_id
puts :symbol.object_id
```

The output once you run the program would then be:

```
>ruby p039symbol.rb
21066960
21066930
132178
132178
>Exit code: 0
```

---

[10] https://zetcode.com/lang/rubytutorial/datatypes/, Zetcode

To sum up, when do we use a string versus a symbol matter: in case the contents (the sequence of characters) of the object are important, use a string. If the identity of the object is more important, use a symbol.

Ruby uses symbols and has a whole Symbol Table to organize them. Symbols may as well be treated as names of instance variables, names of methods, names of classes. So if there is a method called control_movie, there is an automatically produced symbol: control_movie. Ruby is interpreted, so it keeps its Symbol Table handy at all times. You can see what is actually on it at any given moment by calling Symbol.all_symbols.

The symbol object may be unique for each different name but will not refer to a particular instance of the name, for the duration of a program's execution. Additionally, a Ruby symbol cannot be modified at runtime. They are often used as hash keys because we do not need the full capabilities of string objects for a key. In the following example, we can observe some basic operations with Ruby symbols[11]:

```
symbols.rb
#!/usr/bin/ruby

p :name
p :name.class
p :name.methods.size
p "Jane".methods.size

p :name.object_id
p :name.object_id
p "name".object_id
p "name".object_id
```

[11] https://zetcode.com/lang/rubytutorial/datatypes/, Zetcode

The following is used to print a symbol and its class to the console. The class of the symbol would consequentially be Symbol:

```
p :name
p :name.class
```

If you compare the number of methods associated with instances of symbols and strings, a string has more than twice as many methods than a symbol:

```
p :name.methods.size
p "Jane".methods.size
```

Same symbols have the same id. Yet same strings have different ids:

```
p :name.object_id
p :name.object_id
p "name".object_id
p "name".object_id
```

This would be the sample result:

```
$ ./symbols.rb
:name
Symbol
86
183
71068
71068
60
80
```

Symbols may also be used as flags. Let us demonstrate this feature with the following situation. In the below example, light is either on or off, and those both states we are going to define using symbols:[12]

```
symbols2.rb
#!/usr/bin/ruby
light = :on

if light == :on
    puts "The light is on"
else
    puts "The light is off"
end


light = :off

if light == :on
    puts "The light is on"
else
    puts "The light is off"
end
```

The logic of the program depends on the state of the light variable.light = :on. The light is on.

```
if light == :on
    puts "The light is on"
else
    puts "The light is off"
end
```

Since Symbols are more efficient than strings, it is also possible to use them as keys in hash containers. For instance,

---

[12] https://zetcode.com/lang/rubytutorial/datatypes/, Zetcode

in the following script, we have a domains hash and the keys in the hash are symbols:

```
symbols3.rb
#!/usr/bin/ruby
domains = {:sk => "Slovakia", :no =>
"Norway", :hu => "Hungary"}

puts domains[:sk]
puts domains[:no]
puts domains[:hu]
```

Here, keys are used to access values of a hash, and you are expected to print the following three values of a hash:

```
puts domains[:sk]
puts domains[:no]
puts domains[:hu]
```

The output of the example would then become:

```
$ ./symbols3.rb
Slovakia
Norway
Hungary
```

As mentioned before, Ruby comes with lots of things already included in and provides you with tons of tools to use and start running your own application. We have looked at some of the most common data types in Ruby mainly used to represent data, such as numbers, strings, and other values. These are basically the building blocks that you, as a newbie-Ruby programmer will work with, when handling actual data. Now, it is time to unpack the language's control structures, variables, and real-time operators.

## CHAPTER 4

Basics of Language

IN THIS CHAPTER

➢ Reviewing language variables and operator conventions

➢ Analyzing how to apply blocks and iterators correctly

➢ Examining comments and available control structures

In Chapters 2 and 3, we learned the Ruby on Rails installation and configuration process, reviewed data types, and worked with generated files. In this chapter, we will go through the basics of the language and interact with its main features.

It is normal that every developer looks for ways that help in reducing the amount of effort and resources they put into building a new web application, something that can automate the repetitive tasks that are involved in the process of creating a website. Ruby on Rails is just the software for that.

At its most basic—Rails is one of many web frameworks in the world of app programming and web development

DOI: 10.1201/9781003229605-4

that provides developers with a time-saving method for scripting code. This framework acts as a collection of code libraries that give app and web developers readymade solutions for time-consuming tasks such as building menus, tables, or forms on a website. In other words, not only does the Rails web framework reduces the time spend on re-coding repetitive tasks, but—by using Rails code—Rails developers can keep their overall work cleaner, less prone to ineffective code, and easier to troubleshoot when errors do occur. At the same time, Rails subscribes to an overall method of best practices for Rails developers that remove the need to leave behind instructions and strategy for your coding decisions through configuration files in the code you write—instead, Rails developers work from the shared common ground of Rails conventions.

Nevertheless, in order to talk about Rails and its relevance for beginners, it is important to take a step back and understand that it is not just the Rails framework that is beginner-friendly, but the Ruby language it is founded on as well. Basically, Rails IS Ruby, or at least it exists on top of Ruby. This means that understanding Rails will involve learning at least some parts of the Ruby programming language—though nothing beyond basic syntax and configurations.

The Ruby language itself—and not just the Rails web framework—is a great choice as a beginning coding language—it is easy to read and does a lot of the work for you. Other languages, like C, require a lot more code to complete something you can wrap in a few lines with Ruby. At the same time, this is not without some drawbacks—more complicated programming languages ultimately offer more options and control—it works out well for someone just getting started with web development. Ruby is more than capable of carrying you through to an intermediate level of programming. And since Rails is like an extension of Ruby, you can start to learn Ruby on Rails once you have learned Ruby basics. This chapter will start with Ruby variables, blocks, and comments; and later see how you can apply available Ruby control structures to your advantage.

VARIABLES

Ruby variables are memory locations that hold data to be used in the programs. Naturally, Ruby is a part of the family of dynamic languages. Unlike strongly typed languages like Java, C, or Pascal, dynamic languages do not declare a variable to be of a certain data type. Instead of that, the interpreter decides the data type at the moment of the assignment. Variables in Ruby can hold different values as well as different types of values over time.

Moreover, each variable has a different name. These variable names are based on some naming conventions. Yet unlike other programming languages, there is no need to declare a variable in Ruby. Just a prefix is needed to indicate it.

The term variable comes from the fact that variables, in contrast to constants, can take different values over time. In the following example, there is a variable called i. First, it is assigned a value 5, later a different value 7:

```
simple_variable.rb
#!/usr/bin/ruby
i = 5
puts i
i = 7
puts i
```

Ruby Variable Naming Conventions

As already stated, Ruby has some naming conventions for variable identifiers. At the same time, it is a case-sensitive language, meaning that age and Age are two different variable names. But most languages are case sensitive, with the exception of BASIC, which is a case insensitive language. And while it is possible to create different names by changing the case of the characters, this practice is not recommended. The following code example defines two variables: I and I that have different values:

```
case.rb
#!/usr/bin/ruby
i = 5
p i
I = 7
p I
```

The output of the code would then be:

```
$ ./case.rb
5
7
```

Keep in mind that variable names should be meaningful. Thus it is considered a good programming practice to choose descriptive names for variables, making the programs more readable then.

Variable names in Ruby can be constructed from alphanumeric characters and the underscore _ character. But a variable cannot begin with a number. This makes it easier for the interpreter to distinguish a literal number from a variable. Also, variable names cannot begin with a capital letter. If an identifier begins with a capital letter, it is considered to be a constant in Ruby. In the script below, we demonstrate a few valid variable names:

```
valid_variables.rb
#!/usr/bin/ruby

name = "John"
placeOfBirth = "USA"
placeOfBirth = "NY"
favorite_season = "summer"

n1 = 2
n2 = 4
n3 = 7

p name, placeOfBirth, favorite_season
p n1, n2, n3
```

There are five main types of variables supported by Ruby. You already have gone through a brief preview of these variables in the previous chapter and examples as well:

1. Global variables

2. Local variables

3. Class variables

4. Instance variables

5. Ruby pseudo-variables

Variable identifiers normally start with special characters called sigils. A sigil is a symbol attached to an identifier. Variable sigils in Ruby denote variable scope. This is in contrast to Perl, where sigils denote data type. Typical Ruby variable sigils are $ and @.

Not taking Rubyy pseudo-variable into account, we have four variables with different scopes. A scope stands for the range in which a variable can be referenced. You are expected to use special built-in methods to determine the scope of the following variables:

```ruby
sigils.rb
#!/usr/bin/ruby

tree_name = "pine"
$car_name = "Toyota"
@sea_name = "Caspian sea"

class Animal
    @@species = "Dog"
end

p local_variables
p global_variables.include? :$car_name
p self.instance_variables
p Animal.class_variables
```

In this code, a variable without a sigil would be a local variable. A local variable is valid only locally: inside a method, block, or a module:

```ruby
tree_name = "pine"
```

Global variables would be the one starting with $character. They are valid everywhere but the use of global variables should be limited in programs:

```
$car_name = "Toyota"
```

A variable name starting with a @ sigil is an instance variable. This variable is valid inside an object:

```
@sea_name = "Caspian sea"
```

Additionally, we have a class variable. This variable is valid for all instances of a specific class:

```
class Animal
    @@species = "Dog"
end
```

The local_variables gives an array of all local variables defined in a specific context. Our context is Ruby toplevel:

```
p local_variables
```

Similarly, the global_variables produce an array of globals. There is no need to print all globals to the terminal because there are too many of them. Each Ruby script starts with a bunch of predefined variables. Instead of that, you can call the include? method of the array to see if your global is defined in the array:

```
p global_variables.include? :$car_name
```

The pseudo-variable points to the receiver of the instance_ variables method. The receiver in our case is the main, the Ruby top-level execution area:

```
p self.instance_variables
```

At last, we have an array of class variables with the main instance of the Animal class:

```
p Animal.class_variables
```

You can also observe various symbolic names of the variables:

```
$ ./sigils.rb
[:tree_name]
true
[:@sea_name]
[:@@species]
```

Ruby Global Variables

As already mentioned, global variables begin with $. Uninitialized global variables have the value nil and produce warnings with the -w option.

Overall assignment to global variables alters the global status. Yet, it is not advised to use too many global variables as it may make your program cryptic. Here is an example showing the usage of global variable:[1]

```
#!/usr/bin/ruby
$global_variable = 10
```

---

[1] https://www.tutorialspoint.com/ruby/ruby_variables.htm, Tutorialspoint

```
class Class1
   def print_global
      puts "Global variable in Class1 is
#$global_variable"
   end
end
class Class2
   def print_global
      puts "Global variable in Class2 is
#$global_variable"
   end
end


class1obj = Class1.new
class1obj.print_global
class2obj = Class2.new
class2obj.print_global
```

Here $global_variable is a global variable. This will produce the following result:

```
Global variable in Class1 is 10
Global variable in Class2 is 10
```

Please note that it is also possible to access the value of any variable or constant by putting a hash (#) character just before that variable or constant.

Ruby Instance Variables

Instance variables begin with @ and uninitialized instance variables have the value nil and produce warnings with the -w option. We shall illustrate the usage of Instance Variables with the following example:

```
#!/usr/bin/ruby
class Customer
   def initialize(id, name, addr)
      @cust_id = id
      @cust_name = name
      @cust_addr = addr
   end
   def display_details()
      puts "Customer id #@cust_id"
      puts "Customer name #@cust_name"
      puts "Customer address #@cust_addr"
   end
end

# Create Objects
cust1 = Customer.new("1", "Mary", "Times
Apartments, Manhattan")
cust2 = Customer.new("2", "Jane", "New
Empire building, Brooklyn")

# Call Methods
cust1.display_details()
cust2.display_details()
```

Here, @cust_id, @cust_name and @cust_addr are instance variables. This will result in the following output:

```
Customer id 1
Customer name Mary
Customer address Times Apartments,
Manhattan
```

```
Customer id 2
Customer name Jane
Customer address New Empire building,
Brooklyn
```

Ruby Class Variables

Class variables begin with @@ and must be initialized before they can be used in method definitions. Class variables could be shared among descendants of the class or module in which the class variables are defined.

It is important to remember that referencing an uninitialized class variable causes an error; while overriding class variables produce warnings with the -w option. Here is a code sample showing the usage of class variable:

```ruby
#!/usr/bin/ruby
class Customer
   @@no_of_customers = 0
   def initialize(id, name, addr)
      @cust_id = id
      @cust_name = name
      @cust_addr = addr
   end
   def display_details()
      puts "Customer id #@cust_id"
      puts "Customer name #@cust_name"
      puts "Customer address #@cust_addr"
   end
   def total_no_of_customers()
      @@no_of_customers += 1
      puts "Total number of customers: #@@
no_of_customers"
   end
end
```

```
# Create Objects
cust1 = Customer.new("1", ", "Mary", "Times
Apartments, Manhattan")
cust2 = Customer.new("2", "Jane", "New
Empire building, Brooklyn")

# Call Methods
cust1.total_no_of_customers()
cust2.total_no_of_customers()
```

Here @@no_of_customers is a class variable. With it, the code produces the following result:

```
Total number of customers: 1
Total number of customers: 2
```

Ruby Local Variables

Local variables start with a lowercase letter or _. The scope of a local variable ranges from class, module, or def. It is only accessible or has its scope within the block of its initialization. Once the code block completes, the variable has no scope. Assignment to uninitialized local variables also serves as variable declaration. The variables start to exist until the end of the current scope is reached. The lifetime of local variables is determined when Ruby parses the program.

When an uninitialized local variable is referenced, it is interpreted as a call to a method that has no arguments. In the above example, local variables are id, name, and addr.

Ruby Constants

Constants start with an uppercase letter. Constants determined within a class or module can be accessed from within that class or module, and those defined outside a class or module can be accessed globally.

Additionally, constants may not be defined within methods, and referencing uninitialized constant typically results in an error. Making an assignment to a constant that is already initialized results in a warning. Let us see the constants example:

```ruby
#!/usr/bin/ruby
class Example
   VAR1 = 100
   VAR2 = 200
   def show
      puts "Value of first Constant is
#{VAR1}"
      puts "Value of second Constant is
#{VAR2}"
   end
end

# Create Objects
object = Example.new()
object.show
```

In this code, VAR1 and VAR2 are constants. The overall result would then be:

```
Value of first Constant is 100
Value of second Constant is 200
```

Ruby Pseudo-Variables

On the other hand, there are special variables that have the appearance of local variables but act like constants. It is not possible to assign any value to these variables:

- **self:** The receiver object of the current method.

- **true:** Value representing true.

- **false:** Value representing false.

- **nil:** Value representing undefined.

- **__FILE__:** The name of the current source file.

- **__LINE__:** The current line number in the source file.

OPERATORS

Ruby has a built-in modern set of operators. Where operators stand for a symbol that is used to complete different operations. For instance, +, –, /, *.

As you would expect from a modern language, Ruby supports a rich set of operators. For each operator (+ – */% ** & | ^ << >> && ||), there is a corresponding form of abbreviated assignment operator (+= –= etc.). The following are the main types of operators that we shall through one by one:

- Arithmetic operator

- Bitwise operator

- Logical operator

- Ternary operator

- Assignment operator

- Comparison operator

- Range operator

Ruby Arithmetic Operators

Let us assume variable a holds 10 and variable b holds 20, then the following operators mentioned in Table 4.1 would give:

TABLE 4.1   Ruby Arithmetic Operators[2]

Operator	Description	Example
+	Addition – Adds values on either side of the operator.	a + b will give 30
–	Subtraction – Subtracts right hand operand from left hand operand.	a – b will give -10
*	Multiplication – Multiplies values on either side of the operator.	a * b will give 200
/	Division – Divides left hand operand by right hand operand.	b / a will give 2
%	Modulus – Divides left hand operand by right hand operand and returns remainder.	b % a will give 0
**	Exponent – Performs exponential (power) calculation on operators.	a**b will give 10 to the power 20

[2] https://www.tutorialspoint.com/ruby/ruby_operators.htm, Tutorialspoint

Ruby Comparison Operators

Let us assume variable a holds the same 10 and variable b holds 20, then the following operators mentioned in Table 4.2 would give:

TABLE 4.2   Ruby Comparison Operators[3]

Operator	Description	Example
==	Checks if the value of two operands are equal or not, if yes, then condition becomes true.	(a == b) is not true.
!=	Checks if the value of two operands are equal or not, if values are not equal, then condition becomes true.	(a != b) is true.
>	Checks if the value of left operand is greater than the value of right operand, if yes, then condition becomes true.	(a > b) is not true.
<	Checks if the value of left operand is less than the value of right operand, if yes, then condition becomes true.	(a < b) is true.
>=	Checks if the value of left operand is greater than or equal to the value of right operand, if yes then condition becomes true.	(a >= b) is not true.
<=	Checks if the value of left operand is less than or equal to the value of right operand, if yes then condition becomes true.	(a <= b) is true.
<=>	Combined comparison operator. Returns 0 if first operand equals second, 1 if first operand is greater than the second and –1 if first operand is less than the second.	(a <=> b) returns –1.

(Continued)

[3] https://www.w3resource.com/ruby/ruby-comparison-operators.php, W3resource

TABLE 4.2   *(Continued)* Ruby Comparison Operators

Operator	Description	Example
===	Used to test equality within a when clause of a *case* statement.	(1...10) === 5 returns true.
.eql?	True if the receiver and argument have both the same type and equal values.	1 == 1.0 returns true, but 1.eql?(1.0) is false.
equal?	True if the receiver and argument have the same object id.	if aObj is duplicate of bObj then aObj == bObj is true, a.equal?bObj is false but a.equal?aObj is true.

Ruby Assignment Operators

Assume variable a holds 10 and variable b holds 20, then the following operators mentioned in Table 4.3 would give:

TABLE 4.3   Ruby Assignment Operators[4]

Operator	Description	Example
=	Simple assignment operator, assigns values from right side operands to left side operand.	c = a + b will assign the value of a + b into c
+=	Add AND assignment operator, adds right operand to the left operand and assign the result to left operand.	c += a is equivalent to c = c + a
-=	Subtract AND assignment operator, subtracts right operand from the left operand and assign the result to left operand.	c -= a is equivalent to c = c - a

(Continued)

---

[4] https://www.rubyguides.com/2018/07/ruby-operators/, Ruby guides

TABLE 4.3 *(Continued)* Ruby Assignment Operators

Operator	Description	Example
*=	Multiply AND assignment operator, multiplies right operand with the left operand and assign the result to left operand.	c *= a is equivalent to c = c * a
/=	Divide AND assignment operator, divides left operand with the right operand and assign the result to left operand.	c /= a is equivalent to c = c / a
%=	Modulus AND assignment operator takes modulus using two operands and assign the result to left operand.	c %= a is equivalent to c = c % a
**=	Exponent AND assignment operator performs exponential (power) calculation on operators and assign value to the left operand.	c **= a is equivalent to c = c ** a

Ruby Parallel Assignment

Ruby also supports the parallel assignment of variables. This function allows multiple variables to be initialized with a single line of Ruby code. To demonstrate:

- a = 10

- b = 20

- c = 30

This may be easier declared using the following parallel assignment:

- a, b, c = 10, 20, 30

Moreover, Parallel assignment could be helpful for swapping the values held in two variables:

- a, b = b, c

Ruby Bitwise Operators

Bitwise operators operate in regards to bits and perform bit-by-bit operation. To comprehend, assume a = 60; and b = 13; now in the binary format they will be turned into the following:

- a = 0011 1100

- b = 0000 1101

- a&b = 0000 1100

- a|b = 0011 1101

- a^b = 0011 0001

- ~a = 1100 0011

The following is a list of Bitwise operators listed in Table 4.4 are supported by Ruby language.

TABLE 4.4   Ruby Bitwise Operators[5]

Operator	Description	Example
&	Binary AND Operator copies a bit to the result if it exists in both operands.	(a & b) will give 12, which is 0000 1100
|	Binary OR Operator copies a bit if it exists in either operand.	(a | b) will give 61, which is 0011 1101

(Continued)

---

[5] https://www.tutorialspoint.com/ruby/ruby_operators.htm, Tutorialspoint

TABLE 4.4 *(Continued)* Ruby Bitwise Operators

Operator	Description	Example
^	Binary XOR Operator copies the bit if it is set in one operand but not both.	(a ^ b) will give 49, which is 0011 0001
˜	Binary Ones Complement Operator has the effect of "flipping" bits.	(˜a) will give –61, which is 1100 0011 in 2's complement form due to a signed binary number.
<<	Binary Left Shift Operator. The left operands value is moved left by the number of bits specified by the right operand.	a << 2 will give 240, which is 1111 0000
>>	Binary Right Shift Operator. The left operands value is moved right by the number of bits specified by the right operand.	a >> 2 will give 15, which is 0000 1111

Ruby Logical Operators

The following logical operators mentioned in Table 4.5 are supported by Ruby language (assume variable a holds 10 and variable b holds 20):

TABLE 4.5 Ruby Logical Operators[6]

Operator	Description	Example
And	Called Logical AND operator. If both the operands are true, then the condition becomes true.	(a and b) is true.
Or	Called Logical OR Operator. If any of the two operands are non-zero, then the condition becomes true.	(a or b) is true.

(Continued)

---

[6] https://www.rubyguides.com/2018/07/ruby-operators/, Ruby guides

TABLE 4.5   *(Continued)* Ruby Logical Operators

Operator	Description	Example
&&	Called Logical AND operator. If both the operands are non-zero, then the condition becomes true.	(a && b) is true.
||	Called Logical OR Operator. If any of the two operands are non-zero, then the condition becomes true.	(a || b) is true.
!	Called Logical NOT Operator. Use to reverses the logical state of its operand. If a condition is true, then the Logical NOT operator will make false.	!(a && b) is false.
Not	Called Logical NOT Operator. Use to reverses the logical state of its operand. If a condition is true, then the Logical NOT operator will make false.	not(a && b) is false.

Ruby Ternary Operator

There is another operator called Ternary Operator. It is applied to evaluate an expression for a true or false value and then implement one of the two given statements depending upon the result of the evaluation. The conditional operator has the following syntax:

? : - which stands for a standard conditional expression. Thus, if the condition is true ? then choose value X : otherwise, you go with value Y.

Ruby Range Operators

Sequence ranges in Ruby are utilized to create a range of successive values—consisting of a start value, an end value, and a range of values in between as mentioned in Table 4.6.

TABLE 4.6   Ruby Range Operators

Operator	Description	Example
..	Creates a range from start point to end point inclusive.	1..10 Creates a range from 1 to 10 inclusive.
...	Creates a range from start point to endpoint exclusive.	1...10 Creates a range from 1 to 9.

In Ruby, these sequences are built using the ".." and "..." range operators. The two-dot form creates an inclusive range, while the three-dot form activates a range that excludes the specified high value.

Ruby defined? Operators

defined? is an additional operator that takes the form of a method call to set whether or not the passed expression is defined. It returns a description string of the expression or nil in case the expression is not defined. There is multiple usage of defined? operator[7]:

- **Usage 1:** defined? variable # True if variable is initialized
   For Example:

```
foo = 33
defined? foo    # => "local-variable"
defined? $_     # => "global-variable"
defined? bar    # => nil (undefined)
```

---

[7] https://www.tutorialspoint.com/ruby/ruby_operators.htm, Tutorialspoint

- **Usage 2:** defined? method_call # True if a method is defined

    For Example:

```
defined? puts         # => "method"
defined? puts(bar)    # => nil (bar is
not defined here)
defined? unpack       # => nil (not
defined here)
```

- **Usage 3:** # True if a method exists that can be called with super user

    -defined? super

    For Example:

```
defined? super        # => "super" (if it
can be called)
defined? super        # => nil (if it
cannot be)
```

- **Usage 4:** defined? yield # True if a code block has been passed

    For Example:

```
defined? yield    # => "yield" (if
there is a block passed)
defined? yield    # => nil (if there
is no block)
```

Double Colon "::" Operator

The :: is a unary operator that allows: constants, instance methods and class methods set within a class or module, to be accessed from anywhere outside the class or module.

In Ruby, classes and methods may be used as constants too. You just need to prefix the :: Const_name with an expression that returns the appropriate class or module object. If no prefix expression is applied, the main Object class is used by default. To illustrate with an example:

```
MR_COUNT = 0            # constant defined on
main Object class
module Foo
   MR_COUNT = 0
   ::MR_COUNT = 1       # set global count to 1
   MR_COUNT = 2         # set local count to 2
end
puts MR_COUNT           # this is the global
constant
puts Foo::MR_COUNT      # this is the local
"Foo" constant
```

Ruby Operators Precedence

To sum up, it is recommended to review Table 4.7, which presents all operators from highest precedence to lowest (keep in mind that operators with a Yes in the method column are actually methods, and therefore may be overridden):

TABLE 4.7   Ruby Operators Precedence

Method	Operator	Description
Yes	::	Constant resolution operator
Yes	[ ] [ ]=	Element reference, element set
Yes	**	Exponentiation (raise to the power)
Yes	! ~ + -	Not, complement, unary plus and minus (method names for the last two are +@ and -@)
Yes	* / %	Multiply, divide, and modulo

(Continued)

TABLE 4.7   *(Continued)* Ruby Operators Precedence

Method	Operator	Description
Yes	+ -	Addition and subtraction
Yes	>> <<	Right and left bitwise shift
Yes	&	Bitwise "AND"
Yes	^ |	Bitwise exclusive "OR" and regular "OR"
Yes	<= < > >=	Comparison operators
Yes	<=> == === != =~ !~	Equality and pattern match operators (!= and !~ may not be defined as methods)
	&&	Logical "AND"
	||	Logical "OR"
	.. ...	Range (inclusive and exclusive)
	? :	Ternary if-then-else
	= %= { /= -= += |= &= >>= <<= *= &&= ||= **=	Assignment
	defined?	Check if specified symbol defined
	Not	Logical negation
	or and	Logical composition

BLOCKS AND ITERATORS

If you want to master Ruby on Rails be prepared to dive into the logic behind the things we apply every day to understand how they work. In this section, we shall explore the differences between blocks, procs, and lambdas.

In programming languages with first-class functions, functions can be stored in variables and forwarded as arguments to other functions. Or functions can even use other functions as their return values.

Another key feature is closure. Closure stands for a first-class function with an environment. The environment here describes a mapping to the variables that existed when the closure was produced. The closure will then keep its access to these variables, even if they are set in another scope.

Although Rails does not have first-class functions, it still has closures in the form of blocks, procs, and lambdas. Blocks are mostly applied for activating blocks of code to methods, and procs and lambdas permit storing blocks of code in variables.

We have seen previously how Rails defines methods where you can insert a number of statements and then call that method. Similarly, it uses the concept of Block. A block holds chunks of code that you later assign a name to. That code in the block is always enclosed within braces ({}).

Ruby code blocks could also be named closures in other programming languages. A block is always called from a function with the same name as that of the block. Meaning that if you have a block with the name test, then you use the function test to activate this block.

You can also invoke a block by inserting the yield statement consisting of a group of codes that are always enclosed with braces or written between do..end. At the same time, the braces syntax always has the higher precedence over the do..end syntax.

You can script a block in two common ways: multi-line between do and end or inline between braces {}. Both have the same functionality. AS already mentioned, in order to invoke a block, you need to have a function with the same name as the block following the standard syntax:

```
block_name {
    statement1
    statement2
    . . . . . . . . . .
}
```

Now let us see how to call a block by using a simple yield statement. Let us look at an example of the yield statement:[8]

```ruby
#!/usr/bin/ruby
def test
   puts "You are in the method"
   yield
   puts "You are again back to the method"
   yield
end
test {puts "You are in the block"}
```

This will produce the following output:

- You are in the method

- You are in the block

- You are again back to the method

- You are in the block

Additionally, it is also possible to pass parameters with the yield statement. To illustrate with an example:

```ruby
#!/usr/bin/ruby
def test
   yield 7
   puts "You are in the method test"
   yield 50
end
test {|i| puts "You are in the block #{i}"}
```

---

[8] https://www.tutorialspoint.com/ruby/ruby_blocks.htm, Tutorialspoint

This will result in the following data:

- You are in the block 7

- You are in the method test

- You are in the block 50

As you can observe from the above code, the yield statement is written followed by parameters. In the block, you typically place a variable between two vertical lines (||) to accept the parameters. So that in the preceding code, the yield 7 statement passes the value 7 as a parameter to the text block.

Now, to examine the following statement:

```
test {|i| puts "You are in the block #{i}"}
```

Here, the value 7 is received in the variable i. Now, observe the following puts statement:

```
puts "You are in the block #{i}"
```

The output of this puts statement would be:

```
You are in the block 7
```

In case you want to pass more than one parameter, then the yield statement shall turn to become:

```
yield a, b
```

With the block looking like:

```
test {|a, b| statement}
```

Blocks and Methods

Now that you have seen how a block and a method can be associated with each other, you can learn how to invoke a block by using the yield statement from a method that has the same name as that of the block. Thus, you script:

```
#!/usr/bin/ruby
def test
    yield
end
test{ puts "Hello world"}
```

This example is the easiest way to execute a block. The test block you can call by using the yield statement.

However, in case the last argument of a method is preceded by &, then you can pass a block to this method and this block will be assigned to the last parameter. In case both * and & are present in the argument list, then & should come later:

```
#!/usr/bin/ruby
def test(&block)
    block.call
end
test { puts "Hello World!"}
```

This will produce the following output:

```
Hello World!
```

BEGIN and END Blocks

Every Ruby source file can declare blocks of code to be operated as the file that is being loaded (the BEGIN blocks) or the one after the program has finished running (the END blocks). To demonstrate with an example:

```
#!/usr/bin/ruby
BEGIN {
    # BEGIN block code
    puts "BEGIN code block"
}

END {
    # END block code
    puts "END code block"
}
    # MAIN block code
puts "MAIN code block"
```

It is important to note that a program may include multiple BEGIN and END blocks. BEGIN blocks are activated in the order they are encountered while END blocks are implemented in reverse order. When executed, the above program shall present the following information:

- BEGIN code block

- MAIN code block

- END code block

Iterators

Iterator is a term only used in object-oriented language. Iteration means doing one thing multiple times like a loop. Thus, Iterators could be defined as methods supported by collections, where collection stands for random objects that store sets of data members. In Ruby, arrays and hashes can be categorized as collections.

The simplest iterator is the loop method. It is programmed to return all the elements from a collection, one by one. Here we shall briefly discuss two main iterators—each and collect.

Ruby Each Iterator

The each iterator is used to return all the components of an array or a hash through the following standard syntax:

```
collection.each do |variable|
    code
end
```

Here, the code variable executes each element in the collection that could be an array or a ruby hash. To illustrate with an example:

```
#!/usr/bin/ruby
ary = [1,2,3,4,5]
ary.each do |i|
    puts i
end
```

The result of the above code would be the following:

```
1
2
3
4
5
```

It is normal to always associate each iterator with a block as it returns each value of the array, one by one, to the block. The value would then be stored in the variable i and later displayed on the screen.

Ruby Collect Iterator
The collect iterator is used to return all the items of a collection through the following syntax:

```
collection = collection.collect
```

The collect method is not necessarily always associated with a block. Therefore, the collect method returns the entire collection, regardless of whether it is an array or a hash. Take a look at the following example:

```
#!/usr/bin/ruby
a = [1,2,3,4,5]
b = Array.new
b = a.collect
puts b
```

The output of such formula would then be:

```
1
2
3
4
5
```

At the same time, the collect method is not the proper way to handle copying between arrays. There is another method called a clone, which should be applied to copy one array into another array. You generally use the collect method when you need to do something with each of the values to get the new array. For instance, this code produces an array b containing five times each value in a:

```
#!/usr/bin/ruby
a = [1,2,3,4,5]
b = a.collect{|x| 5*x}
puts b
```

This will generate the following output:

```
5
10
15
20
25
```

Procs

A proc is simply an instance of the Proc class, which consists of a code block to be executed, and can be put in a variable. In order to create a proc, you should call Proc.new and pass it a block in the following manner:

```
proc = Proc.new { |n| puts "#{n}!" }
```

Since a proc can be placed in a variable, it can also be passed to a method just like any other standard argument. In that case, there is no need to use the ampersand (&), as the proc is passed explicitly:

```
def run_proc_with_random_number(proc)
  proc.call(random)
```

```
end
proc = Proc.new { |n| puts "#{n}!" }
run_proc_with_random_number(proc)
```

If you do not want to create a proc and pass that to the method, you can use Ruby's ampersand parameter syntax that was mentioned earlier and use a block instead:

```
def run_proc_with_random_number(&proc)
  proc.call(random)
end
run_proc_with_random_number { |n| puts
"#{n}!" }
```

Here, keep in mind that the & is added to the argument in the method. With that, it will convert a passed block to a Proc object and store it in a variable in the method scope. Even though it could be useful to have the proc in the method in some instances, the conversion of a block to a proc might result in a performance hit. Thus, whenever possible, try to use implicit blocks instead.

In addition, symbols, hashes and methods can also be converted to procs using their #to_proc methods. A frequently seen application of this is passing a proc created from a symbol to a method in the following manner:

```
[1,2,3].map(&:to_s)
[1,2,3].map {|i| i.to_s }
[1,2,3].map {|i| i.send(:to_s) }
```

This example presents three equivalent ways of calling #to_s on each element of the array. In the first one, a symbol, prefixed with an ampersand, is passed, which automatically converts it to a proc by calling its #to_proc method. The last two show what that proc might potentially look like.

```
class Symbol
  def to_proc
    Proc.new { |i| i.send(self) }
  end
end
```

This simplified example was brought to show the detailed implementation of Symbol#to_proc: the first method returns a proc which takes one argument and sends the self-variable to it. Since self is the symbol in this context, it activates the Integer#to_s method.

Lambdas

To put it simply, lambdas are basically procs with some distinguishing characteristics. At the same time, they are similar to methods in two ways: they can enable a great number of arguments passed when they are activated, and they use standard returns.

When calling a lambda without having an argument, or passing an argument to a lambda that does not expect it, Ruby throws an ArgumentError:

```
irb> lambda (a) {a }.call
ArgumentError: wrong number of arguments
(given 0, expected 1)
 from (irb):8:in 'block in irb_binding'
 from (irb):8
 from /Users/jeff/.asdf/installs/
ruby/2.3.0/bin/irb:11:in '<main>'
```

Additionally, a lambda treats the return keyword the same way a method would do: if calling a proc, the program yields control to the code block in the proc. So, if the proc returns, the current scope returns. If a proc is called inside a function and calls return, the function immediately returns as well:

```
def return_from_proc
  a = Proc.new { return 5 }.call
  puts "This will never be printed."
End
```

The next function will yield control to the proc, so when it returns, the function returns. Calling the function in this example will never print the output and return 5:

```
def return_from_lambda
  a = lambda { return 5}.call
  puts "The lambda returned #{a}, and this
will be printed."
End
```

If you are using a lambda, it will be printed. Calling return in the lambda might feel like calling return in a method, so the a variable is populated with 5 and the line is printed to the console.

Now that you have reviewed some basics about blocks, procs, and lambdas, we may look back and try to summarize the comparison.

Blocks are utilized extensively in Ruby for passing bits of code to functions. By inserting the yield keyword, a block can be simply passed without having to convert it to a proc.

Yet when using parameters prefixed with ampersands or passing a block to a method results in a proc in the method's context. To put it simply, procs act like blocks, but they can be stored in a variable. Lambdas are the same as procs but act like methods, meaning they enable arity and return as methods instead of in their parent scope.

COMMENTS

Ruby comments are non-operable lines in a program. A programmer scripts them to describe their code so that others who look at the code will comprehend it in a better way. The interpreter naturally omits these lines; therefore, they are not implemented during the program execution.

It is considered good practice to insert comments before classes and methods as well any segment of code that may be difficult or confusing. Comments should be added to provide background information or to interpret difficult code. Other notes that simply state what the next line of straightforward code does are not only obvious but simply add clutter to the file. Therefore, it is important to take care and not to use too many comments and to be sure the comments made in the file are useful and suggestive to other programmers.

There are two types of Ruby comments: Single line comment multi-line comment

A single-line comment starts with # character and they extend from # to the end of the line as follows:

```
#!/usr/bin/ruby -w
# This is a single line comment.
puts "Hello, Ruby!"
```

When operated, the above program produces the following result:

```
Hello, Ruby!
```

When it comes to multiple lines comment, you can use =begin and =end syntax in the following manner:

```
#!/usr/bin/ruby -w
puts "Hello, Ruby!"
=begin
```

This is a part of the multiline comment, and it is possible to add as many lines as you like. But =begin and =end should come in the first line only.

```
=end
```

When implemented, the above program produces the following output:

```
Hello, Ruby!
```

It is also essential to check and make sure trailing comments are far enough from the code and that they are easily set apart. If more than one trailing comment is in a block, you are expected to align them in the following way:

- **@counter:** # keeps track times page has been accessed

- **@siteCounter:** # keeps track of times all pages have been accessed

The Shebang

Hopefully, you will be able to pay attention and notice that all Ruby programs start with a comment that begins with #!. This is called a shebang and is mostly used on Linux, Unix, and OS X systems. When you run a Ruby script, the shell (such as bash on Linux or OS X) will look for a shebang at the first line of the file. The shell will then use the shebang to search for the Ruby interpreter and execute the script.

The preferred Ruby shebang is #!/usr/bin/env ruby, though you may also see #!/usr/bin/ruby or #!/usr/local/bin/ruby.

CONTROL STRUCTURES

Ruby programming language provides certain statements in addition to loops, conditionals, and iterators, which are useful to edit and modify the flow of control in a program.

To be precise, these statements are a segment of code that runs one after another until the condition is true and when the condition becomes false, then code gets simply terminated. The following are the statements that can change the control flow in a Ruby program:

- break statement

- next statement

- redo statement

- retry statement

- return statement

- throw/catch statement

break Statement

In Ruby, break statement is used to end a loop when the condition is true. Break statement is also used in while loop because in while loop the output is displayed until the condition is true, in case the condition is false the loop terminated.

The break statements are mainly executed by break keyword and could be added to for, while, and case-control statements.

The original syntax is: break
For example:[9]

```
# Ruby program to demonstrate break
statement
#!/usr/bin/ruby
i = 1
  # using while loop
while true
    if i * 6 >= 30
# using break statement
        break

    # ending of if statement
    end
    puts i * 6
    i += 1
 # ending of while loop
end
```

---

9 https://www.javatpoint.com/ruby-break-and-next-statement#:~:text=Ruby%20
Break%20Statement,called%20from%20inside%20the%20loop., javatpoint

The output would be the following:

```
6
12
18
24
```

In the above example, the break statement is mainly applied to end the execution of the while loop when the condition if i * 6 >= 30 becomes true. If that is not done, the loop goes up to infinite.

next Statement

In Ruby, the next statement is mostly applied to move to the next iterator of a given loop. The next statement is similar to the continue statement in C and Java language. When the next statement is added no other iteration will be conducted. Typically, the next statement is inserted to for and while loop.

The basic next Syntax is: next

To explain with an example:

```ruby
# Ruby program to show next statement
#!/usr/bin/ruby
  # using for loop
for t in 0...10
     # using if statement
   if t == 5 then
       # using next statement
     next
    # ending of if
   end
     # displaying values
   puts t
  # end of for loop
end
```

The final result would then be displayed:

```
0
1
2
3
4
6
7
8
9
```

Keep in mind that in the above program, 5 will not be printed in the output because of the next statement. Since here at 5 next statement will force to skip it and continue from next statement in program.

redo Statement

The redo statement is utilized to start over the current iteration of a loop or the iterator. It might seem that the redo and next statement are similar, but next statement always transfers the control to the end of the loop where the statement after the loop can start to operate, but redo statement transfer the control back to the top of block or loop so that iteration can start all over.

The standard syntax is: redo

To illustrate with the following example:

```
# Ruby program to show the redo statement
  # defining a variable
val = 0
```

```
# using while loop which should give
# output as 0,1,2,3 but here it will
# output as 0,1,2,3,4
while(val < 4)

# Control returns here when
# redo will execute
puts val
val += 1

# using redo statement
redo if val == 4
  # ending of while loop
end
```

The logical output of the above code would then be:

```
0
1
2
3
4
```

In the above program, the redo statement will transfer the control to puts val, which is the first expression of the while loop. It is not wired to retest the loop condition, nor it is set to fetch the next element from the iterator. Thus, here while loop will print 0,1,2,3,4 instead of 0,1,2,3.

retry Statement

retry statement is used to restart an iterator depending on a certain condition or any method invocation. In other words, the retry statement transfers the control at the beginning. However, you are most likely not going to use this statement often its only works until Ruby version 1.8. It has been removed from Ruby version 1.9 onwards because it is considered an outdated feature. So it will hardly be used in an online IDE's because it mostly uses versions above 1.8.

Standard syntax is: retry

To understand the retry usage, take a look at the following example:

```ruby
# Ruby program to demonstrate the retry
statement
# variable
var = 7

# Iterate 7 times from 0 to 7-1
var.times do |val|

# display iteration number
puts val

# If we've reached 6
if val == 6

# Decrement val and user won't
# reach 6  next time
var = var - 1

# Restart the iteration
# using retry statement
retry
```

```
# end of if
end
# end of do..end
end
```

As a result, the output would be:

```
0
1
2
3
4
5
6
0
1
2
3
4
5
```

As you might have noticed, when the control goes to retry statement, it transfers that control to var.times do |val|. With that, the value of the var variable is updated at 5. Meaning the user will not reach 6 next time and retry statement will not have to run again.

return statement

return statement is applied to exit from a method, with or without a value. It returns a value to its caller at all times. It is a very flexible option—if there is no expression used with the return statement, then it always returns the value of the method as nil. A list of expressions after the return statement has to be separated by the comma(,). In this case, the value of the method will converse to an array containing the values of those specified expressions. A very simple example of the statement would be:

```ruby
# Ruby program to show the return statement
#!/usr/bin/ruby
# defining a method 'geeks'
def geeks

    # variables of method
    val1 = 20
    val2 = 35
# returning multiple values
return val1, val2

# this statement will not execute
puts "Hello Geeks"

# end of the method
end

# variable outside the method to
# store the return value of the method
value = geeks

# displaying the returned values
puts value
```

The output would then be:

```
35
20
```

In this example, method geeks has a return statement which return val1 and val2 to its caller. Here value comes as the variable which holds the returned values. The key point is that the statement puts "Hello Geeks" after the return statement does not implement it since statements after the return statement cannot run inside a method.

throw/catch Statement

throw and catch are used to describe a multilevel, complex control structure. throw is applied to break the running loop and shift the control outside of the catch block. The useful thing about throw is that it can break out of the current loop or methods or we can say it can cross any number of features. And catch mainly determines a specific segment of code which causes to exit by the throw block. To illustrate with an example:

```ruby
# Ruby program to show the throw/catch
statement
# for altering the control flow

# defining a method
def lessNumber(num)

    # using throw statement
    # here 'numberError' is its label
    throw :numberError if num < 100

    # displaying result
    puts "Number is Greater than 100!"
end

# catch block
catch :numberError do

    # calling method
    lessNumber(110)
    lessNumber(180)
```

```
    # exits catch block here
    lessNumber(77)
    lessNumber(34)
end
  puts "Outside Catch Block"
```

Output:

```
Number is Greater than 100!
Number is Greater than 100!
Outside Catch Block
```

In the above code, 110 is forwarded to method lessNumber to check whether it is greater than 110 or not. 110 is greater than 100 so statement will eventually print out on display and the next statement of catch block will run. After that, 180 is offered to the method call, which is checked and greater than 100, so the statement will print out on screen. However, as soon as 77 is proposed which is less than 100 throw: numberError forces the catch block to exit and all the statements skip out, and the last statement "Outside Catch Block" will be displayed. Therefore, as soon as the condition becomes false throw makes the catch block exit the catch block from overall implementation.

To summarize, in this chapter, we have discussed the Ruby on Rails basics and learned how to work with its main components. In particular, we have demonstrated how you can manage variables, blocks, and iterators, as well as comments and control structures. In the next chapter, we shall focus on running the database through object-relational mapping and active record basics.

## CHAPTER 5

Working with Database

IN THIS CHAPTER

> ➤ Discovering Object-Relational mapping on Ruby on Rails

> ➤ Outlining the role of SQL in programming

> ➤ Learning about Active Record Basics

When you are creating an app with Ruby on Rails development, chances are, you will have to manage the massive amount of data. And in a project as such, you cannot simply store data in the notepad—without solid structure, it will quickly become an uncontrollable clutter. Especially if you are building a backend in Ruby on Rails, creating a database

DOI: 10.1201/9781003229605-5

that will take care of data-based processes and keep the app's information structured is essential. Therefore, in this chapter, we shall talk about the most popular databases in Ruby on Rails web development, introduce you to the process of consolidating them, and outline the best practices.

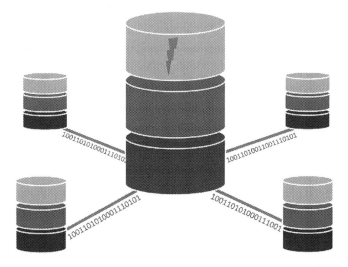

Ruby on Rails is a Web application framework made for developing Web applications. And in your application, if you expect or need a user to enter information through a Web form, you require a database to store all that information. In Rails framework, the database table has a plural name (ending with "s"), and the primary key in the database is known as id and auto-incremented. To retrieve stored information from the database, Rails utilizes a component named ActiveRecord that operates as a bridge between the database and Ruby code. ActiveRecord is an

Object-Relational Mapping layer that comes with Rails. It follows standard layer rules such as:

- Columns map to hold object attributes

- Rows map to contain objects

- Tables map to enclose classes

Each ActiveRecord object has Create, Read, Update, and Delete methods for database access. This capacity allows Ruby on Rails applications to perform straightforward mappings between applications objects and database tables. Moreover, ActiveRecord does not always need to use SQL in most cases even if it is perfectly compatible with different databases such as MySQL, SQLite, and PostgreSQL. Yet regardless of the database you are using, the ActiveRecord method format remains the same.

If you find yourself in charge of a Rails app for the first time, there are a couple of areas where you really do not want to have any issues:

- **Data Integrity:** Is all the data in your database reliable?

- **Database Performance:** Do your queries return in an appropriate amount of time?

As far as these points are concerned, database transactions (and their ActiveRecord counterparts) are great tools for avoiding these problems. Transactions are typically used when you need to ensure data integrity, even if your web app crashes in the middle of a request. Properly applied, they can speed queries and guarantee data safety. Another noteworthy thing about transactions is that they are actually executed by the database. You can use them anywhere you use PostgreSQL/MySQL.

To be specific, transactions are protective blocks where SQL statements are only fixed if they can all succeed as one atomic action. The simplest example of such action could be a transfer between two accounts where you can only have a deposit if the withdrawal succeeded and vice versa. Transactions preserve the integrity of the database and guard the data against program errors or database collapse. Basically, you should make use of transaction blocks whenever you have a number of statements that should be implemented together, or not at all.

Transactions have a well-structured life cycle. At any given time, your transaction should be in a certain state:

- **Active:** Your data operations are being executed.

- **Partially Committed:** Your data operations have been completed successfully, but modifications have not been committed to the database, and cannot be accessed outside of the transaction.

- **Committed:** Your data operations have been completed successfully and locked any changes in the database.

- **Failed:** Some error has occurred, which caused the database to stop the transaction. The database has not been reloaded at this point.

- **Aborted:** Your database has been reloaded after a failure, and the transaction is complete.

Now, let us take the previous example of the bank transaction between two accounts and convert it into a code:

```
ActiveRecord::Base.transaction do
  sender.debit_account(amount) if sender.
sufficient_balance(amount)
  credit_amount = convert_currency(amount,
recipient)
  perform_transfer(recipient, credit_
amount, sender)
  transfer.update_status
end
```

Here, you are expected to call the transaction method on the ActiveRecord::Base class and pass it a block. Every database operation that takes place within that block will be forwarded to the database as a transaction. If any kind of sudden error happens inside the block, the transaction will be aborted, and no changes will be made to the database.

```
ActiveRecord::Base#transaction
```

In the above code segment, you are calling the transaction method on the ActiveRecord::Base class. You might find it useful when dealing with controller or service code. Also keep in mind that in general, every ActiveRecord model has to have a transaction method. Imagine that you have a Transfer class that inherits from ActiveRecord. The following would be the case:

```
Transfer.transaction do
  ...
end
my_model_instance#transaction
```

Similarly, every instance of your ActiveRecord models also has its own transaction method:

```
transfer = Transfer.new(…)
transfer.transaction do
  …
end
```

And, because the transaction method is an ordinary Ruby method, you can reference it in the standard model definitions:

```
class Transfer < ApplicationRecord
  def perform(...)
    self.transaction do
      ...
    end
  end
end
```

In case you would be looking to manually abort a transaction and prevent any of its modifications from being written to the database, it is possible to activate the ActiveRecord::Rollback method:

```
ActiveRecord::Base.transaction do
  @new_user = User.create!(user_params)
  @referrer = User.
find(params[:referrer_id])
  raise ActiveRecord::Rollback if @
referrer.nil?
  @referrer.
update!(params[:reference_record])
end
```

Meanwhile, any unhandled exception that occurs during the transaction will also cause it to be aborted. There are two common ways to raise these exceptions: by using ActiveRecord methods ending with an exclamation mark: save!, update!, destroy! Or by manually raising an exception in ActiveRecord, when a method name ends with an exclamation mark, raising an exception on failure. Let us imagine we have a transaction that involves creating a new user account, while also updating the record of another user (the referrer):

```
ActiveRecord::Base.transaction do
  @new_user = User.create!(user_params)
  @referrer.
update!(params[:reference_record])
end
```

Here, the inserted create! and update! methods will raise an exception if something goes wrong.

Also, in case you were to use the create and update methods (without the exclamation mark), they would indicate a failure via their return value, and the transaction would keep running. It is also possible that if you wanted to, you could always check the return value yourself and "manually" raise an exception if necessary:

```
ActiveRecord::Base.transaction do
  @new_user = User.create(user_params)
  raise ActiveRecord::RecordInvalid unless
@new_user.persisted?
end
```

Typically, it does not really matter what kind of exception you raise. Any exception class can be used to abort the transaction. But it is still important to remember to rescue the exception in the following manner:

```
def create_referrer_account
  ActiveRecord::Base.transaction do
      raise ActiveRecord::RecordInvalid if
@referrer.nil?
  rescue ActiveRecord::RecordInvalid =>
exception # handle error here...
  end
end
```

The transactions we have reviewed so far only let you work with a single database. And since most Rails apps only use one database that works out perfectly. However, if you want to ensure data integrity across multiple databases, you can do so by nesting ActiveRecord transactions. In the example below, it has been scripted that the User and Referrer models point to different databases:

```
User.transaction do
  @new_user = User.create!(user_params)
  Referrer.transaction do
    @referrer.
update!(params[:reference_record])
  end
end
```

In case any parts of the inner transaction fail, it will cause the outer transaction to be aborted. Yet since nested transactions can be difficult to get right for beginners, it is recommended to try your best to avoid them.

In programming, just like in our lives, very few things come free of consequences. Transactions give us a great way to ensure data integrity, but they have a few potential drawbacks:

- **Performance:** Using a transaction generally consumes more resources on the database server than the raw queries.

- **Complexity:** When overused, transactions can make your code more complex and therefore harder to comprehend.

For instance, when you use a transaction in Rails, it ties up one of your database connections until all the code in your transaction block finishes running. If the block holds something heavy, such as an API call, you would be tying up your database connection for an unreasonable amount of time:

```
ActiveRecord::Base.transaction do
  User.create!(user_params)
  SomeAPI.do_something(u)
end
```

Overall, the key principle of using transactions well could be to use them only when you really need them. Even though transactions give developers the ability to write SQL statements in the right way, it also has a great responsibility attached to it—one that should not be abused by initiating transactions everywhere.

In addition to what we have learned, it would also be useful to ask yourself whether there is a need to handle more than one SQL statement at all. And if the answer is yes, make sure you are raising and rescuing the errors as was shown above.

OBJECT-RELATIONAL MAPPING ON RUBY ON RAILS

Object-relational mapping in computer science is a programming technique for transmitting data between incompatible type systems with the use of object-oriented programming languages. The result of this, in effect, is the creation of a "virtual object database" that can be accessed from within the programming language.

The Object part is the one you use with your programming language (Ruby object in our case). The Relational component is a Relational Database Manager System (simply a database). And finally, the Mapping part is where you do a bridge linking your objects with your tables. There is a variety of free and commercial packages available that offer object-relational mapping, although some programmers choose to construct their own mapping tools.

In object-relational Rails data mapping, data-management tasks act on objects that stand as non-scalar values. For instance, consider an address book entry that has a single person along with zero or more phone numbers and zero or more addresses. This could be easily converted in an object-oriented application by a "Person object" with an attribute/field to contain each data item that the entry comprises involves: the person's name, a list of phone numbers, and a list of addresses. The generated list of phone numbers would itself contain "PhoneNumber objects" and others. Each such address-book entry would be treated as a single object by the programming language (it is typically referenced by a single variable holding a pointer to the object). Multiple methods can be linked with the object, such as methods to return the preferred phone number, or the home address.

To compare, many widely-used database products such as SQL database management systems are not object-relational and can only hold and manipulate scalar values such as integers and strings placed within tables. The programmer is expected then to either convert the object values into groups of simpler values for storage in the database and convert them back upon retrieval, or only use simple scalar values within the program. However, both approaches typically have a problem of translating the logical representation of the objects into a standard form that is capable of being stored in the database while preserving the characteristics of the objects and their relationships so that they can be reloaded as objects when needed. Thus, only if you implement such storage and retrieval procedures, the objects would then be persistent.

Using object-relational mapping, the properties and relationships of the objects in an application can be easily stored and retrieved from a database without writing SQL statements directly and with less database access code. This data management style acts as a completely ordinary library scripted in your language that encapsulates the code necessary to manipulate the data, so you do not have to use SQL anymore, but directly use an object of your language.

Active Record

It is not possible to discuss object-relational mapping without mentioning the Active Record pattern. To put it simply, Active Record is a specific approach to accessing data in a database. Let us explain it this way: an ordinary database table or view is wrapped into a class, and an object instance is tied to a single row in the table. After the creation of an object, a new row is added to the table upon save. Any object loaded gets its data from the database. When an object is updated, the corresponding row in the table is also updated. The wrapper class then executes accessor methods or properties for each column in the table or view.

So if you need to get an array containing a listing of all the users, instead of scripting code to initiate a connection to the database, then going through SELECT * FROM users query, and converting those results into an array, you can just type User.all and Active Record shall give you that array filled with User objects that you can apply as you like.

Moreover, it does not actually matter which type of database you are using (as long as you have set up the config/database.yml file), Active Record will even out all the differences between those databases for you so there is nothing to worry about. You just have to focus on writing code for your application, and Active Record can handle the details of connecting you to your database. It also means that if you move from one database to another, you do not actually need to modify any major application code, just a few configuration files.

The overall relationship between Rails and a database is pretty straightforward—you need to store information about your projects, so you create a database table called project 1,2,3, etc. You want to be able to access that data from your application, so you produce a model called Project, which is really just a Ruby file that inherits from Active Record and thus gets to use all the conventional methods like all and find or create. One table has to correspond with one model which inherits from Active Record.

Let us demonstrate it with the following example: you have College class and one way to structure it would be to implement Active Record to Class object in the following way:

```
class College < ActiveRecord::Base
  has_many :students
end
class Student < ActiveRecord::Base
  belongs_to :college
end
```

Now, in your migration it is possible to add a foreign key for referencing another table:

```
class CreateColleges <
ActiveRecord::Migration
  def change
    create_table :colleges do |t|
      t.string :name
      t.timestamps
    end
  end
end
class CreateStudents <
ActiveRecord::Migration
  def change
    create_table :students do |t|
      t.string :name
      t.integer :college_id
      t.timestamps
    end
  end
end
```

As a result of the above code, Student and College would stand as classes with corresponding tables in the database. Objects of the class Student and College would correspond to rows in the table and essential attributes of Student and College such as name associate with columns from the row:

```
2.2.2 :003 > college = College.find(17)
  College Load (0.5ms)  SELECT
"colleges".* FROM "colleges" WHERE
"colleges"."id" = $1 LIMIT 1  [["id", 17]]
 => #
2.2.2 :004 > college.students
  Student Load (0.7ms)  SELECT "students".*
FROM "students" WHERE "students"."college_
id" = $1  [["college_id", 17]]
 => #
2.2.2 :005 >
```

Here, make sure to notice that college.students were converted into SQL queries, to get all students having college_id as "17".

Student Load (0.7ms) SELECT "students".* FROM "students" WHERE "students"."college_id" = $1 [["college_id", 17]]

The above segment could be introduced if you are planning to use ActiveRecord with its has_many, belongs_to, has_one methods for which corresponding SQL queries are fired.

This framework wraps around a relational database and should be viewed as a great programming technique for converting data between incompatible systems in object-oriented programming languages. It also ensures that you do not have to call a database yourself. Meaning that with the object-relational mapping, there is no need to set the SQL format data, as such:

```
UPDATE table_name
SET column1 = value1, column2 = value2, …
WHERE condition;
or
CREATE TABLE table_name (
column1 datatype,
column2 datatype,
column3 datatype,
```

Instead, all you really need to do is inherit ActiveRecord::Base and use has_many, has_one relationships.

Advantages

There are many advantages to object-relational mapping dealing with databases. In Ruby on Rails, the technique is known to be:

- **Database Independent:** There is no need to write code in a particular database.

- **Reduces Code:** The framework provides the concept of abstraction, which means there is no need to repeat the same code again.

- **Rich Query Interface:** It allows the developer to clear out the complex semantics of SQL.

As for ActiveRecords, it is a powerful framework of object-relational mapping in Ruby on Rails. Using the functionality provided by this module, you can:

- Establish a connection to a database

- Produce database tables

- Specify associations between tables that correspond to associations between the Ruby classes

- Initiate an association between Ruby classes/objects/ attributes and the tables/rows/columns in the underlying database

- Perform complex operations on Ruby ActiveRecord objects

Disadvantages
The model is helpful in Ruby code completion and in running frameworks to reduce workload. However, there are certain drawbacks in some areas, such as:

- **Overhead Issues:** The framework consumes more memory than other relational databases and increases central processing unit usage.

- **Performance Issues:** Particular actions, such as inserting a large data, updating it, or deleting it are slower if executing through object-relational mapping. Native SQL queries could be used to handle these actions more efficiently.

WHAT ABOUT SQL?

Let us rewind to some fundamental points at first. A database is a file that collects organized information. A key principle of a database is to maintain order within its system and databases group objects according to set values, characteristics, and hierarchy. Normally, databases use formal structure and models to demonstrate relationships between data.

Databases come as SQL and NoSQL. SQL stands for Structured Query Language, and it uses tables to store data and preserve relations between them. Each table is associated with at least one other table, and all information, therefore, becomes a part of a defined structure. Because of this emphasis on relations, SQL databases are often called relational.

On the other hand, NoSQL databases do not use Structured Query Language. Unlike relational databases that apply the same language, no matter which management system you operate in, NoSQL are very dependent on tools. For instance, if you ever build with Mongo-DB, one of the most popular non-relational databases, you will have to learn its logic and terminology. And later when switching to another non-SQL tool, you would be expected to relearn most aspects from scratch.

Typically, deciding between SQL and NoSQL databases is the first step for many. Both have certain advantages worth noting:

- **SQL databases:** have a precise order. If a file is not described well or has errors, the database will immediately send a notification. Additionally, all relations follow the same logic that is easy to scale and manage.

- **NoSQL databases:** are more flexible, which is why they are most preferred for managing qualitative data. If information cannot be easily broken down into tables, setting up a non-relational database might be the solution. NoSQL databases are easier to set up, but at the same time, they require constant maintenance—you need to avoid duplication, file errors, and establish relations all by yourself.

At this point of your learning curve, it is recommended to opt for relational databases because they are more scalable. In the long run, it would be easier to recruit developers, add new data, and operate data flow.

Nevertheless, the choice of a database does not depend that heavily on the framework. Let us review the most common options:

- **PostgreSQL:** it is one of the most cost-efficient, flexible, and versatile SQL databases out there. One of its main advantages is the ability to hold large amounts of data and complex operations. It has a reputation for being a strict database since it does not let developers input non-sense data and always follows strict data quality constraints. However, that is what makes data quality management easy in the long run, especially in complex projects.

- **SQLite:** it is supported by Ruby on Rails by default as a highly efficient database. It is also known as an internal database, used mainly to cover the needs of production and testing. It is a common one for local projects and internal builds. Additionally, it is often used to set up the basic data structure and then get replaced for a more powerful alternative.

- **MySQL:** it could possibly be the most popular SQL database right now. Its requirements are less stringent than those of PostgreSQL and because of that, it is easier to set up and manage.

In this section, we shall talk about all three of them, starting with PostgreSQL, since as a beginner, you should learn how to add elaborate functionality and make changes to various data structures.

How to Make a PostgreSQL Database in Ruby

To start, you need to set up a Cloud Server on Linux and install and open PostgreSQL. With that, you need a basic background of Ruby on Rails and a proper understanding of Ruby's syntax. The database commands here will be given from a user perspective– so to be sure you could use the same account that you used for the installation of Ruby on Rails.

- **Step 1:** Creating a PostgreSQL user
  You need to create a user account on PostgreSQL. This profile will then be synchronized with the Ruby on Rails page and used to issue back-and-forth commands. Here is the necessary command:

  ```
  sudo -u postgres createuser -s
  [username]
  ```

- **Step 2:** Create a password for your user
  To define access and protect database security, you would be asked to assign a password to your user. It does not necessarily have to be the same as for the

application's compatibility Ruby on Rails account. You can open PostgreSQL prompt with sudo -u postgres psql

And then enter a command to set a password: \ password [username]

After that you should enter the command again to confirm the password: \password [username]

- **Step 3:** Setting PostgreSQL database with Ruby on Rails Next, it is necessary to build a bridge between your database management system and Rails application. For that, create a Ruby on Rails application rails new [application name] -d postgresql. The -d flag indicates to Rails that you will be running PostgreSQL to work with the application. Now both tools have the permission to interact.

  Once that is done, access the directory with Rails application and create a new database there. To open a directory, enter cd application-name. To create a database, enter nano config/database.yml. After that, you should be getting the following message:

  - # The specified database role being used to connect to postgres.

  - # To create additional roles in postgres, see "$createuser --help."

  - # When left blank, postgres will use the default role. This is

  - # the same name as the operating system user that initialized the database.

  - #username: application-name2

Here, do not forget to update your user name. In the last row, edit the username to match the one that corresponds to your Rails and PostgreSQL user and add a password to your account. This way, it will be stored in the system and you will not lose access credentials.

- **Step 4:** Creating a database
  In order to create a new database table in Ruby on Rails, you need to use rake comments applied specifically to create, migrate, and manage databases. To create a database, enter the following:

```
rake db:create.
```

- **Step 5:** Testing a database inside the application
  To check if the integration was successful, open the application with your browser and go to the application directory to enter the following command:

```
bin/rails s --binding=0.0.0.0
```

If the integration was successful, you should see the following message:

```
[user@localhost my-app]$ bin/rails
server
=> Booting Puma
=> Rails 5.0.0.1 application starting
in development on http://localhost:3000
=> Run "rails server -h" for more
startup options
Puma starting in single mode...
```

```
* Version 3.6.0 (ruby 2.3.1-p112),
codename: Sleepy Sunday Serenity
* Min threads: 5, max threads: 5
* Environment: development
* Listening on tcp://localhost:3000
```

This basically means that the application is running with no errors. If you want to double-check still, you can go to http://your-IP:3000/ (instead of your-IP enter the numbers that correspond to your address). And if you established the Ruby connect to PostgreSQL database, you should see the Rails welcome message.

How to Integrate MySQL With Ruby on Rails

To start with, you need to prepare installed MySQL, open the root password from MySQL, and run Ruby on Rails. After that you may process with the following guideline:

- **Step 1:** Adding MySQL gem to your RoR code
  In order to connect MySQL to Ruby on Rails, enter these commands:

  ```
  sudo apt-get update
  sudo apt-get install MySQL-client
  libmysqlclient-dev
  ```

  With that you will be connected to the MySQL client files, now you need to download a gem that will be used by Ruby on Rails to interact with a database. To do that, enter:

  ```
  gem install mysql2
  ```

- **Step 2:** Preparing the Ruby on Rails application
  Now you have to write comments in your app with Ruby to connect to the database. For that, enter the d-flag to allow MySQL's access to the app:

```
rails new [application name] -d MySQL
```

You could better define and secure database access by rooting a password which the application will attach a password to your username. Simply enter MySQL -u root –p and this command will give you the right to input a password.

- **Step 3:** Editing App's Config File
  Now, we can proceed to creating a new Ruby on Rails application and connecting it to your MySQL database.
  To start with, open the directory with the application by entering cd my-app. Next, open the database configuration file in the same directory with the following command:

```
nano config/database.yml
```

In this file, you should look to set and confirm the password to your application and database: password: [MySQLpassword]. But instead of MySQL password, try to enter your own combination (for instance AFOR230893).

After that you can create MySQL database on Ruby on Rails, using the same rake database command we mentioned earlier:

```
rake db:create
```

- **Step 4:** Check the application
  It is possible to verify the compatibility of an application with a database by closing the app config file and opening the application in your browser. To proceed with that, in the app's directory, enter the following:

```
bin/rails s --binding=0.0.0.0
```

If verified, you should see the following message:

```
[user@localhost my-app]$ bin/rails server
=> Booting Puma
=> Rails 5.0.0.1 application starting
in development on http://localhost:3000
=> Run "rails server -h" for more
startup options
Puma starting in single mode...
* Version 3.6.0 (ruby 2.3.1-p112),
codename: Sleepy Sunday Serenity
* Min threads: 5, max threads: 5
* Environment: development
* Listening on tcp://localhost:3000
Use Ctrl-C to stop
```

For additional verification, you could visit http://IP-address:3000. Here, remove 'IP-address' and enter the numbers that correspond to your IP instead. If the integration was successful, the link will redirect you to Ruby's welcome page.

How to Integrate SQLite With Ruby on Rails?
As previously stated, SQLite is a default Ruby database, in other words, it comes in the package with Ruby itself.

Therefore, its integration takes only several commands. Specifically, the Linux package of Ruby comes with SQLite, so you can use commands to regulate it. On Windows, you need to install DevKit first. After that, you can call the database with a command:

```
gem install sqlite3
```

At the same time, the Linux distribution does not require install commands—you can start entering the rake commands for Ruby database immediately.

For Fedora, you should enter:

```
dnf install rubygem-sqlite3
rubygem-sqlite3-doc
```

For Ubuntu, insert the following:

```
apt install ruby-sqlite3
```

Best Practices of Ruby Database Development

In case you are not just getting started with Ruby on Rails database development but already have it set, you might be interested in practices that could alter your efficiency. The following points apply to most databases and cover general principles rather than database-specific technicalities:

- **Integrate databases as early as possible:** The main idea of a database is to maintain data. They have various features for organizing, sorting information, searching for errors, and removing entire structures. Sometimes, independent developers choose to handle small data-related tasks with Ruby or Ruby on Rails alone. So, the first recommendation would be, if you want to carry out some data-based process on Ruby, consider that it definitely can be accomplished better in a database.

- **Reduce the number of calls to a database:** Ruby on Rails and Active Record offer simpler shortcuts for developers to work with databases. You could be tempted at times to create many small datasets because they are easier to set up and organize. Yet then, they are forced to send multiple data queries to run each of these sets. However, once the application is activated, the amount of data would only be growing. And in case your page sends multiple calls to a Ruby on Rails database, it will become really slow. When an application hosts thousands of users simultaneously, servers might not be able to process that many requests.

  The best practice here is to not forget to insert includes and joins to request multiple data in one query. Nevertheless, if you just request for data without using proper syntax, you might be stuck in a loop and block the entire operation.

- **Use indexes to quickly find data:** This one is pretty straightforward: in order to avoid going through more data than necessary, it is recommended to add reference indexes into your columns.

- **Adopt consistent datatypes early on:** In case you want to write code that will be easy to maintain, the best way to do it is to build and maintain a strong adherence to data types within your team. It is recommended to form and follow consistent rules for naming and hierarchy, and your codebase will become much more approachable. In particular, it is better to take time exploring the lesser-known data types that will help you to structure your data in many frameworks.

Typical Mistakes of Ruby on Rails Database Development

When you work with large amounts of data, you have to consider the best development practices carefully. One additional move, misplaced or missing command can result in unexpected delays. Manageable at first, these problems will pile up and wreck your performance quality.

Even if you do not have that much Ruby on Rails development experience, it might help to look through this section paying attention to the given technical terms. Even without a profound understanding, it will provide you with key principles of what issues developers typically deal with while integrating Ruby on Rails databases.

- **Getting multiple data with one query:** Often, specialists prefer incorporating a lot of data in a single query to speed up the development face and script shorter code. To achieve that, they end up creating a loop, and instead of processing data once, the application goes through the same process multiple times.

  To gain more control over performance and avoid over-fetching, it is always better to split data requests into different queries. Also, it is important to constantly look out for unwanted loops. You could let the application know that all data should be fetched with a minimal number of queries by including the "includes" command.

- **Differentiating between LENGTH, COUNT, and SIZE:** One of the basic operations in the database is calculating how many records it holds in total. Essentially, there are three ways of tackling this task but not many know how to properly differentiate between the following options:

  - **LENGTH:** Used to load all the records from the Ruby on Rails database first and determine their size.

  - **COUNT:** Applied to define the number of records by running an SQL query.

  - **SIZE:** Works only for loaded records and calls for the LENGTH method to check the queries' size.

  To put it simply, COUNT is the fastest one between them, but it gives you less information. The choice between LENGTH and SIZE depends on whether the files have been downloaded or not. If you are not sure, use Size.

  To illustrate COUNT with the following example:

```
users = User.where(hotel_id: 10)
users_count = users.size
users.each do |user|
        puts "#{user.full_name}"
end
SELECT COUNT(count_column) FROM (SELECT
1 AS count_column FROM "users"
WHERE "users"."hotel_id" = 10)
subquery_for_count
SELECT  "users".* FROM "users" WHERE
"users"."hotel_id" = 10
```

- **Calculating on Ruby's side:** Determining where to take and process data-related calculations (such as calculating the size of all records) has a huge impact on performance. Unfortunately, the difference between the two is often unsaid—which results in serious processing delays.

The general standard is to perform calculations on SQL size instead of Ruby. Even if the code gets more extensive, but the performance speed improves by 5–10 times. To demonstrate with an example:[1]

```
#1 - Processing on Ruby's side
companies = Company.includes(:users).
limit(100)
companies.each do |company|
    puts company.users.map(&:hotel_id).
uniq.count
end
```

The return of a benchmark: 1.771338 seconds

```
#2 - Processing on SQL's side
companies = Company.limit(100)
.  select('companies.*, companies_
hotels.hotels_count as hotels_count')
.  joins('
    INNER JOIN (
      SELECT companies_users.
company_id,
        COUNT(DISTINCT users.hotel_id)
as hotels_count
```

---

[1] https://syndicode.com/blog/getting-started-with-ruby-on-rails-database-development/, Syndicode

```
      FROM users
      INNER JOIN "companies_users" ON
"users"."id" =
"companies_users"."user_id"
      GROUP BY companies_users.
company_id
    ) as companies_hotels ON companies_
hotels.company_id = companies."id"
  ')
companies.each do |company|
  puts company[:hotels_count]
end
```

The return of a benchmark: 0.127908

In bigger projects, these differences accumulate and become an impact factor in deciding final performance speed and over user experience.

In this section of Ruby on Rails database development, we summarized the best practices and resources for getting started with database integration and management. To sum up, integrating databases is one of the most significant decisions for any backend—because the database will end up managing most of your data-based process.

ACTIVE RECORD BASICS

Active Record is the M in the MVC or Model-View-Controller model—which is the layer of the system responsible for handling business data and logic. Active Record facilitates the creation and use of business objects whose data requires persistent storage in a database. It is an implementation of the Active Record pattern, which itself is a key component of an Object-Relational Mapping system.

In Active Record, objects have both persistent data and behavior which comes with that data. Active Record follows the principle that ensuring data access logic as part of the object will encourage users to learn how to write to and read from the database. Using Object-relational Model, the properties and features of the objects in an application can be easily stored and retrieved from a database without inserting SQL statements directly and with less overall database access code.

Possessing basic knowledge of relational database management systems and structured query language is useful in order to fully master Active Record. Active Record can offer several handy mechanisms, the most important being the ability to:

- Represent models and their data.

- Create associations between these models.

- Save and show inheritance hierarchies through related models.

- Validate models before they get to the database.

- Complete database operations in an object-oriented manner.

When scripting applications using other programming languages or frameworks, it may be necessary to include a lot of configuration code. This is particularly true for Object-Relational Model frameworks but, if you follow the conventions adopted by Rails, you will be expected to write very little configuration (in some cases no configuration at all) when building Active Record models. The idea is that if you modify your applications in the very same way most of the time, then this becomes the default way. As a result, the explicit configuration would be needed only in those cases where you cannot follow the standard convention.

Naming Conventions

By default, Active Record produces certain naming conventions to find out how the mapping between models and database tables should be created. Rails automatically pluralize your class names to search for the respective database table. So, for a class Image, you should have a database table called Images. The Rails pluralization mechanisms are very fundamental, being capable of pluralizing (or singularizing) both regular and irregular words.

When using class names composed of two or more words, the model class name should follow the Ruby conventions, using the CamelCase form, while the table name must contain the words separated by underscores. For instance:

1. **Model Class:** Singular with the first letter of each word capitalized (BreakfastClub).

2. **Database Table:** Plural with underscores separating words (breakfast_clubs).

To illustrate with the following examples:[2]

Model/Class	Table/Schema
1. Article	articles
2. LineItem	line_items
3. Deer	deers
4. Mouse	mice
5. Person	people

---

[2] https://guides.rubyonrails.org/active_record_basics.html, Ruby on Rails

Active Record also uses naming conventions for the columns in database tables, depending on the purpose of these columns:

- **Foreign keys:** These fields should be named following the pattern singularized_table_name_id (item_id, order_id). These are the fields that Active Record will search for when you create associations between your models.

- **Primary keys:** Active Record will use an integer column named id as the table's primary key (bigint for PostgreSQL and MySQL, integer for SQLite). When using Active Record Migrations to create your tables, this column will be automatically created.

In addition, there are also some optional column names that provide additional characteristics to Active Record instances:[3]

- **created_at:** Automatically gets set to the current date and time when the record is first created.

- **updated_at:** Automatically gets set to the current date and time whenever the record is created or updated.

- **lock_version:** Adds optimistic locking to a model.

- **type:** Specifies that the model uses Single Table Inheritance.

- **(association_name)_type:** Stores the type for polymorphic associations.

---

[3] https://guides.rubyonrails.org/active_record_basics.html, Ruby on Rails

- **(table_name)_count:** Applied to cache the number of belonging objects on associations. For instance, a comments_count column in an Article class that has many instances of Comment will cache the number of existent comments for each article.

Even if these column names are optional, they are in fact reserved by Active Record. You are free to use these reserved keywords if you want some extra functionality.

Creating Active Record Models

In order to create Active Record models, you just need to subclass the ApplicationRecord class in the following way:

```
class Product < ApplicationRecord
end
```

This will produce a Product model, mapped to a products table at the database. By running this, you will also gain the ability to map the columns of each row in that table with the attributes of the instances of your model. Suppose that the products table was created using an SQL (or one of its extensions) statement like this:[4]

```
CREATE TABLE products (
  id int(11) NOT NULL auto_increment,
  name varchar(255),
  PRIMARY KEY  (id)
);
```

---

[4] https://guides.rubyonrails.org/active_record_basics.html, Ruby on Rails

The script above creates a table with two columns: id and name. Each row of this table creates a certain product with these two parameters. Therefore, you would be able to script code like the following:

```
p = Product.new
p.name = "Some Book"
puts p.name # "Some Book"
```

At the same time, what if you need to establish a different naming convention or need to use your Rails application with a legacy database. In that case, it is possible to override the default conventions.

ApplicationRecord inherits from ActiveRecord::Base, which determines the number of helpful methods. You can use the ActiveRecord::Base.table_name= method to pick out the table name that should be used:

```
class Product < ApplicationRecord
  self.table_name = "my_products"
end
```

Once you do so, you will have to define manually the class name that is containing the fixtures (my_products.yml) using the set_fixture_class method in your test definition:

```
class ProductTest < ActiveSupport::TestCase
  set_fixture_class my_products: Product
  fixtures :my_products
  end
```

It is also possible to override the column that should be used as the table's primary key using the ActiveRecord::Base. primary_key= method:

```
class Product < ApplicationRecord
  self.primary_key = "product_id"
end
```

Here, keep in mind that Active Record does not support using non-primary key columns named id.

CRUD: Reading and Writing Data

CRUD is a term that stands for the four verbs we use to operate on data: Create, Read, Update and Delete. Active Record automatically creates methods to let an application read and manipulate data stored within its tables.

Active Record objects can be made from a hash, a block, or have their attributes manually issued after creation. The new method will return a new object while create will return the object and save it in the database. For instance, let us take a model User with attributes of name and occupation, the create method call will create and save a new record into the database:

```
user = User.create(name: "Mary",
occupation: "Modern Artist")
```

By adding the new method, an object can be instantiated without being saved:

```
user = User.new
user.name = " Mary "
user.occupation = " Modern Artist "
```

A call to user.save will commit the record to the database. At last, if a block is provided, both create and new will give away the new object to that block for initialization:

```
user = User.new do |u|
  u.name = " Mary "
  u.occupation = " Modern Artist "
end
```

Additionally, Active Record has a rich API for accessing data within a database. Below are a few examples of various data access methods provided by Active Record:[5]

```
# return a collection with all users
users = User.all

# return the first user
user = User.first

# return the first user named Mary
david = User.find_by(name: ' Mary ')

# find all users named Mary who are Modern
Artists and sort by created_at in reverse
chronological order
users = User.where(name: ' Mary ',
occupation: ' Modern Artist').
order(created_at: :desc)
```

---

[5] https://guides.rubyonrails.org/active_record_basics.html, Ruby on Rails

When Active Record object has been retrieved, its key features can be modified and it can be saved in the database using the following code:

```
user = User.find_by(name: ' Mary ')
user.name = ' Mary '
user.save
```

An alternative for the above code would be to use a hash mapping attribute names to the desired value, like this:

```
user = User.find_by(name: ' Mary ')
user.update(name: 'M')
```

This could possibly be the most useful when updating several attributes out there. Yet, on the other hand, if you would like to update several records in a set, you may find the update_all class method quite helpful:

```
User.update_all "max_login_attempts = 3,
must_change_password = 'true'"
```

In addition, once retrieved an Active Record object can be sent to destroy, which automatically removes it from the database:

```
user = User.find_by(name: ' Mary ')
user.destroy
```

In case you would like to delete several records in a code combination, you could use destroy_by or destroy_all method:

```
# find and delete all users named Mary
User.destroy_by(name: ' Mary ')

# delete all users
User.destroy_all
```

Validations

Active Record lets you validate the state of a model before it gets scripted into the database. There are a few methods that you can try to check your models and validate that an attribute value is not empty, is indeed unique and not already in the database, and has a specific format.

Validation is a very significant matter to consider when submitting to the database, so the methods save and update take it into account when running: they return false when validation fails and they do not actually complete any operations on the database. All of these have a suitable counterpart (that is, save! and update!), which are more fixed in that they raise the exception ActiveRecord::RecordInvalid if validation fails. A quick example to demonstrate:

```
class User < ApplicationRecord
  validates :name, presence: true
end

irb> user = User.new
irb> user.save
=> false
irb> user.save!
ActiveRecord::RecordInvalid: Validation
failed: Name can't be blank
```

Migrations

Migrations stand for a convenient way to update your database schema over time in a sustainable manner. You could think of any given migration segment as being a new "version" of the database. A schema starts off with nothing in it, and each migration edits it to add or get rid of tables, columns, or entries. Active Record knows how to alter your schema along its own timeline, bringing it from any random point it is in the history to the latest version. Active Record will also update your db/schema.rb file to match the up-to-date structure of your database. Let us take a look at the following example of a migration:[6]

```
class CreateProducts <
ActiveRecord::Migration[6.0]
  def change
    create_table :products do |t|
      t.string :name
      t.text :description

      t.timestamps
    end
  end
end
```

This particular migration adds a table called products with a string column called name and a text column called description. A primary key column called id will also be added implicitly, as it is the default primary key for all Active Record records. Additionally, the timestamps macro adds two columns, created_at and updated_at that are special columns automatically managed by Active Record.

It is important to remember that you have to define the change that you want to happen moving forward in time. Before this migration is run, there will be notable. After, the table will exist. Active Record will then reverse this migration, and when you roll this migration back, it will remove the table.

---

[6] https://guides.rubyonrails.org/active_record_migrations.html, Ruby on Rails

On databases that enable transactions with statements that modify the schema, migrations are included in a transaction. If the database does not support this feature, then once a migration fails, the parts of it that succeeded will not be rolled back. You will then be forced to roll back the changes that were made manually.

However, there are certain queries that cannot run inside a transaction. If your adapter supports Data Definition Language transactions, then you can use disable_ddl_transaction! to disable them for a single migration. But if you wish for migration to complete something that Active Record does not know how to reverse, you can activate the following reversible:

```
class ChangeProductsPrice <
ActiveRecord::Migration[6.0]
  def change
    reversible do |dir|
      change_table :products do |t|
        dir.up   { t.change :price, :string }
        dir.down { t.change :price,
:integer }
      end
    end
  end
end
```

As an alternative, you can apply up and down definitions instead of change:

```
class ChangeProductsPrice <
ActiveRecord::Migration[6.0]
  def up
```

```
   change_table :products do |t|
     t.change :price, :string
   end
 end

 def down
   change_table :products do |t|
     t.change :price, :integer
   end
 end
end
```

Migrations are typically saved as files in the db/migrate directory, one for each migration class. The name of the file is of the form YYYYMMDDHHMMSS_create_products.rb, that is to state that a UTC timestamp identifies the migration followed by an underscore, followed by the name of the migration.

The name of the migration class (CamelCased version) is supposed to match the latter part of the file name. For example, 20080906120000_create_products.rb should stand for class CreateProducts while 20080906120001_add_details_to_products.rb should determine AddDetailsToProducts. Rails applies this timestamp to indicate which migration should be run and in what order, so if you are dragging a migration from another application or generating a file yourself, you could see its position in a particular order.

Naturally, calculating timestamps might seem like a tedious task, so Active Record provides a generator to handle making it for you:

```
$bin/rails generate migration
AddPartNumberToProducts
```

The above code will then produce an appropriately named empty migration:

```
class AddPartNumberToProducts <
ActiveRecord::Migration[6.0]
  def change
  end
end
```

At the same time, this generator can accomplish much more than append a timestamp to the file name. Based on naming conventions and additional arguments, it can also significantly support the migration. If the migration name is of the form "AddColumnToTable" or "RemoveColumnFromTable" and is followed by a list of column names and types, then the generator shall create statements containing the appropriate add_column and remove_column.

Writing a Migration

Once you have created your migration using the generator, you could now work on its content. Creating a table seems like the first thing you might need. The create_table method is one of the most useful, but most of the time, it will already be generated for you by using a model or scaffold generator. A general syntax would be:

```
create_table :products do |t|
  t.string :name
end
```

which results in a products table with a column called name. By default, create_table will also create a primary key called id. You can modify the name of the primary key with the :primary_key option or, if you do not want a primary key at all, you can use the option id: false. In another case, if you need to pass database-specific options, you can insert an SQL fragment in the :options option. For instance:

```
create_table :products, options:
"ENGINE=BLACKHOLE" do |t|
  t.string :name, null: false
end
```

To note, the above will later append ENGINE=BLACKHOLE to the SQL statement applied to create the table.

Also, you can use the :comment option with any description for the table that will be forwarded to the database itself and can be accessed with database administration tools, such as MySQL Workbench or PgAdmin III. Yet with that, it is highly recommended to specify comments in migrations for applications with large databases as it would help other developers to understand the data model and review full documentation.

Creating a Join Table

The migration method create_join_table generates an HABTM (has and belongs to many) join table. A typical code would be:

```
create_join_table :products, :categories
```

which results in the creation of a categories_products table with two columns called category_id and product_id. These columns have the option :null set to false by default.

However, it could easily be overridden by modifying the :column_options option in the following manner:

```
create_join_table :products, :categories,
column_options: {null: true}
```

Typically, the name of the join table comes from the union of the first two arguments provided to create_join_table, in alphabetical order. And in case you need to customize the name of the table, you could do that by providing a :table_name option:

```
create_join_table :products, :categories,
table_name: :categorization
as a result of this, you shall have a
categorization table.
```

create_join_table also supports a block, which you can apply to use indices (which are not provided by default) or any other additional columns:

```
create_join_table :products, :categories
do |t|
  t.index :product_id
  t.index :category_id
end
```

Changing Columns

Like the remove_column and add_column Rails also offers the change_column migration method:

```
change_column :products, :part_number,
:text
```

This changes the column part_number on products table to be a :text field. Here, remember that change_column command is irreversible.

Besides change_column, the change_column_null, and change_column_default methods are used specifically to modify a not-null constraint and default values of a column like that:

```
change_column_null :products, :name, false
change_column_default :products, :approved,
from: true, to: false
```

The above code sets :name field on products to a NOT NULL column and the default value of the :approved field from true to false. It is also possible to write the above change_column_default migration as change_column_default :products, :approved, false, but unlike the previous example, this would turn your migration to an irreversible one.

Column Modifiers

The following built-in column modifiers can be applied when creating or changing a column in the following instances:[7]

- **limit:** to set the maximum size of the string/text/binary/integer fields.

- **Precision:** to define the precision for the decimal fields, representing the total number of digits in the number.

- **scale:** to set the scale for the decimal fields, representing the number of digits after the decimal point.

---

[7] https://guides.rubyonrails.org/active_record_migrations.html, Ruby on Rails

- **polymorphic:** to add a type column for belongs_to associations.

- **null:** allows or disallows NULL values in the column.

- **default:** allows setting a default value on the column. In case you are using a dynamic value (such as a date), the default will only be calculated the first time (on the date the migration is applied).

- **comment:** to add a comment for the column.

Using the Change Method

The change method is the original way of writing migrations that works for the majority of cases, where Active Record knows how to reverse the migration automatically. As of now, the change method supports only the following list of migration definitions:[8]

- add_column

- add_foreign_key

- add_index

- add_reference

- add_timestamps

- change_column_default (must supply a :from and :to option)

- change_column_null

---

[8] https://guides.rubyonrails.org/active_record_migrations.html, Ruby on Rails

- create_join_table

- create_table

- disable_extension

- drop_join_table

- drop_table (must supply a block)

- enable_extension

- remove_column (must supply a type)

- remove_foreign_key (must supply a second table)

- remove_index

- remove_reference

- remove_timestamps

- rename_column

- rename_index

- rename_table

- change_table is also reversible, as long as the block does not call change, change_default or remove.

- remove_column is reversible if you supply the column type as the third argument. Provide the original column options too, otherwise Rails can't recreate the column exactly when rolling back:

- remove_column :posts, :slug, :string, null: false, default:

- remove_column :posts, :slug, :string, null: false, default:

Please note that if you are going to need to use any other methods, you should apply reversible or write the up and down methods instead of using the change method.

Active Record and Referential Integrity

The Active Record way states that intelligence is kept in your models, not in the database. As such, components such as triggers or constraints, which push some of that intelligence back into the database, are not heavily applied.

Validations such as validates :foreign_key, uniqueness: true are one way in which models can enable data integrity. The :dependent option on associations lets models to automatically remove child objects if the parent is destroyed. Like anything that runs on the application level, these cannot guarantee referential integrity, and so some people alter them with foreign key constraints in the database.

Even though Active Record does not provide all the tools for operating directly with such features, the execute method can be applied to implement arbitrary SQL. The key purpose of Rails' migration feature is to give away commands that modify the schema using a sustainable process. Migrations can also be used to add or modify data that is useful in an existing database that cannot be destroyed or recreated, such as the following production database:

```
class AddInitialProducts <
ActiveRecord::Migration[6.0]
  def up
    5.times do |i|
      Product.create(name: "Product ##{i}",
description: "A product.")
    end
  end
```

```
  def down
    Product.delete_all
  end
end
```

In order to add initial data after a database is created, Rails offers a built-in "seeds" feature that is used to speed up the process. This is especially helpful when reloading the database frequently in development and test environments. To activate this feature, fill up db/seeds.rb with some Ruby code, and run bin/rails db:seed:

```
5.times do |i|
  Product.create(name: "Product ##{i}",
description: "A product.")
end
```

This is considered to be the most suitable and clean way to set up the database of a blank application.

Old Migrations

The above-mentioned db/schema.rb or db/structure.sql are used to get the overall capture of the current state of your database and is the authoritative source for modifying that database. This same solution makes it possible to get rid of old migration files.

Once you delete migration files in the db/migrate/directory, any environment where bin/rails db:migrate was run when those files still existed will contain a reference to the migration timestamp specific to them inside an internal Rails database table named schema_migrations. This table will be useful for keeping track of whether migrations have been implemented in a specific environment. And if you run the bin/rails db:migrate:status command, which presents the status (up or down) of each migration, you should see ********** NO FILE ********** displayed next to any deleted migration file which was once executed on a specific environment but is no longer available in the db/migrate/directory.

To summarize this chapter, we have discussed the most popular databases in Ruby on Rails web development, introduced you to the process of consolidating them, and offered some of the best practices on how to handle Rails object-relational mapping. In the last chapter, we shall examine Rails in association with modern IDE as well as see what editors, both paid and free can handle Rails code.

## CHAPTER 6

Ruby on Rails IDEs

IN THIS CHAPTER

➤ Learning about the concept of IDE

➤ Creating a list of commercial and free IDEs for Ruby on Rails

➤ Installing and working with Middleman generator

An integrated development environment (IDE) is software for creating applications that integrates basic developer tools into a single graphical user interface. A typical IDE usually consists of the following key items:

- **Source code editor:** A text editor that assists you in scripting software code with functions such as syntax highlighting with visual notes, providing language-specific auto-completion features, and scanning for bugs as code is built.

DOI: 10.1201/9781003229605-6

- **Local build automation:** Function that automates simple, repeated tasks as part of creating a local software for use by the developer, such as compiling computer source code into binary code, setting binary code, or completing automated tests.

- **Debugger:** A program for checking other programs that can graphically point at the location of a bug in the original code.

An IDE is great since it lets developers start programming new applications quickly as multiple features do not need to be repeatedly and manually edited and integrated as part of the creation process. There is also no need to spend hours learning how to apply and modify different tools when every utility is represented in the same workbench. This can be especially helpful for onboarding new staff who can rely on an IDE to match the teams' speed of working on standard tools and workflows. As a matter of fact, most features of IDEs are meant to save time, like intelligent code completion and automated code generation, which removes the necessity to script full character lines over and over again.

Other useful IDE features are meant to assist you to structure the overall workflow and solve any issues that might occur along the way. IDEs parse code as it is written, so bugs caused by technical errors are picked out in real-time. And since such utilities are represented by a single user interface, developers can activate actions without switching between applications. Syntax highlighting is also common in most IDEs, which uses visual notes to maintain correct grammar in the text editor. Some IDEs also like to include class and object browsers, as well as class hierarchy layouts for certain languages.

At the same time, it is totally possible to develop applications without an IDE, or for each developer to try and build their own IDE by manually merge various utilities with a lightweight text editor like Vim or Emacs. The main benefit of this approach is the ultra-customization and authority it provides. In an enterprise setting, though, the time saved, environment standardization, and automation characteristics of modern IDEs usually outweigh other reasoning.

Nowadays, most enterprise development teams go for a pre-configured IDE that suits their specific case requirements, so the question here is not whether to adopt an IDE, but rather which IDE to choose. There are various technical and business applications for IDEs, which only means there are many commercial and open-source IDE options on the market. Normally, the most important differentiating features between IDEs are the following:

- **The number of supported languages:** Some IDEs are focused only on one language and are a perfect match for a specific programming case. To take IntelliJ, for instance, that is known primarily as a Java IDE. Other IDEs have a wider array of supported languages all in one, like the Eclipse IDE which supports Java, XML, and Python.

- **Supported operating systems:** A developer's operating system might pose a serious limitation when deciding which IDEs are viable and if the application being developed is intended for an end-user with a certain operating system like Android or iOS, this may be an additional constraint.

- **Automation features:** Even though most IDEs include the three essential features of a text editor, build automation, and debugger, many also have support for additional features like refactoring, code search, continuous integration, and real-time deployment tools.

- **Impact on system performance:** An IDE's memory imprint should be important when considering if you want to run any memory-intensive applications.

- **Plugins and extensions:** Some IDEs include the option to customize workflows to match your tech requirements and preferences.

MOBILE DEVELOPMENT IDEs

Most likely, every industry has been impacted in one way or another by the rising popularity of apps made for smartphones and tablets, forcing many companies to develop mobile apps in addition to standard web apps. One of the key points in mobile application development is platform choice. Therefore, if a new application is designed for use on iOS, Android, and a web page, it may be advised to start with an IDE that offers cross-platform support for various operating systems.

CLOUD IDEs

IDEs that are provided as a cloud-based Software-as-a-Service can offer you a great number of unique benefits compared to the local development setting. To start with, as with any SaaS offering, there is no need to download software and modify local environments and dependencies, meaning that developers can start contributing to projects quicker. This also ensures a certain level of standardization across team members' environments, which can prevent any common workflow problems. In addition, because the development environment is centrally managed, no code resides on an individual developer's computer, which can secure intellectual property and foresee any security concerns.

The effect of processes on local machines is also quite different from what cloud services can offer. Processes like running code and testing projects are typically compute-intensive, which means developers are probably unable to continue using workstations while the process is active. Cloud IDE can dispatch long-running processes without taking over all of the compute resources of a local machine. Cloud IDEs are also typically platform agnostic, enabling connection to different cloud providers.

Depending on the programming language for which it works, the application of IDE might differ. Yet, there are still some basic rules of it that have been explained below:

- It is possible for the programmer to navigate through a type without having to think about the project with an IDE.

- When the user is typing and some error shows up, it will give away warnings.

- The Ruby on Rails developer can use the hyperlinks and easily navigate through all the tasks using an IDE.

- Based on the previous codes, it lets programmers generate codes automatically.

- An IDE can help to add some appropriate imports as well as organize those imports.

- As the codes run from the same window, IDE makes the running of unit tests quite easy.

It is also worth mentioning that the program gets to directly run time exception from the error details or navigate directly to compile-time error using IDE. Now that we have seen what an IDE means and checked out some of its basic uses, we can see some of the best IDEs which can be used for Ruby on Rails development for your project.

PAID IDE OPTIONS

Ruby on Rails usage statistics proves that it is indeed a great and popular backend framework for web development companies since scripting code in Ruby is easier compared to the rest of the programming languages. As a matter of fact, Ruby gained its popularity only after the Ruby on Rails framework became prevalent. And now developers across the globe use Rails for rapid web development of user-focused, high traffic websites, and applications. The process of programming in Rails is faster than the rest of the languages and frameworks, partly due to the object-oriented foundation of Ruby and the extensive collection of open-source code accessible within the community.

The most dedicated Rails community provides Ruby Gems for almost all sorts of assignments. These collections are open-source and have absolutely no licensing costs, therefore making it so dissimilar to other commercial development frameworks. Apart from cost-saving, the framework is also known to be highly productive, readable, and self-documenting. These characteristics enhance productivity, as there is less requirement to write out specific documentation. Plus, the self-documentation makes it easier for developers to pick up random, ongoing projects. Additionally, the Rails conventions make it possible for developers to switch between diverse Rails projects.

It is a fact that every project is standardized and set to abide by the same coding practices and flow. Rails is mostly preferred for rapid application development, as this framework offers almost effortless accommodation of any alterations. Rails also has built a particular emphasis on testing and has a sufficient testing framework. Owing to these attributes, the framework is mainly applied by start-ups and businesses who prioritize quick and secure results.

Basically, Ruby on Rails IDE is all you require to start your programming mission with the Ruby on Rails web framework. There are several IDEs that are available in today's market, both paid and free, and choosing one might be time-consuming. To help you with that, in this section we shall provide you with a list of the best commercial IDE for Rails development:

1. **RubyMine:** RubyMine is an IDE that upgrades your productivity level in every aspect of Rails projects development – from drafting and debugging code to testing and deploying a completed application. Let us go through a brief overview of some of the most important features available in RubyMine:

   - **Smart editor:** This editor allows you to write error-free code faster with type-aware code completion, smart code inspections, live templates, and intention actions.

- **Code completion:** You can code faster with auto-completion. It runs as you type, suggesting a list of matching variables, methods, and keywords. This completion works for Ruby and Rails, JavaScript, CoffeeScript, CSS, and Sass.

- **Refactoring:** Refactoring your code typically means fast and safe renaming and delete refactoring. You can complete all kinds of refactorings with RubyMine: extract variables, parameters, methods, or superclasses, introduce constants, and many more. All the refactorings are Ruby on Rails aware, and renaming a controller will also rename the related helper, views, and tests.

- **Code styling and formatting:** With this feature, you can configure and use a consistent code style for any language. After you set the formatting for indents, spaces, and aligning rules, you can share it with your teammates. RubyMine automatically applies the configured code style as you script. It can also reformat whole files all at once.

- **Documenting code:** With this feature, it is possible to view documentation in a popup, create missing tags using intention actions, and check their validity. RubyMine utilizes YARD annotations for better code review, allowing it to suggest relevant results in code completion and parameter settings for methods.

- **Live templates:** Live templates let you type less when you use the most common pattern outlines in your code. The same feature enables you to customize the existing templates or create your own if needed.

- **Code inspections and quick-fixes:** You will always be the first to see if there are any errors and system breakdowns, such as unreachable code, incorrect call argument count, unused variables, and others. You could then resolve these problems automatically by applying quick fixes suggested by the IDE. Just like that RubyMine upgrades your productivity with Rails and natively supports all major web development practices.

- **Rails-aware code maintenance:** RubyMine supports Rails concepts and enhances code insight features. For example, Autocompletion works for DB fields, associations, and methods determined by names and resource routes.

  Similarly, Rails-aware rename refactoring takes into account names of controllers, views, tests, and helpers. RubyMine then offers support for editing these views, with braces, folding, syntax highlighting, and code completion. In case you are using HAML or Slim views, you can find syntax highlighting for the injected Ruby code as well as coding assistance for HTML code inside the IDE.

- **MVC-based navigation:** You can easily navigate between Rails controllers, actions, views, models, database schemas, and tests simply by using the Navigate Related Symbol command.

- **Rails generators:** It is permitted to add new Rails entities, such as models, controllers, and migrations, to your project with an interface that provides quick and context-sensitive access to Rails generators.

- **Rails internationalization support:** You can create or edit local properties using intention actions right in the editor, to be able to run an inspection to search for missing keys, preview localized values, and others.

- **Model dependency diagram:** Using a model dependency diagram, you can take a bird's-eye view of your project models with their components to analyze the project structure and navigate to the code you need.

- **Ruby tools:** RubyMine offers great and sustainable integration with all the popular Ruby tools, including Rubocop, Bundler, and Rake.

- **Bundler integration:** You can manage various gem dependencies for your application right inside the IDE using the Bundler integration and run Bundler commands right from the Run Anything popup.

- **Version managers and gem sets support:** These tools enable you to quickly switch between the different Ruby versions installed using version managers, such as RVM, rbenv, asdf, and chruby. Additionally, you can also work with RVM and rbenv gemsets in the IDE.

- **Rake support:** You can run any Rake task in your project using the Run Anything popup (double Ctrl). Or it is also possible to complete tasks right from the editor using gutter icons.

- **Rubocop integration:** With Rubocop integration feature, you can dix Rubocop offenses right inside the IDE and check the entire project and display all RuboCop warnings in a single report.

- **Built-in IRB and Rails consoles:** Using the IRB and Rails consoles, it is possible to interact with your application without ever having to leave the IDE.

- **Testing:** With RubyMine, you can generate, run, and manage your tests with ease.

- **User interface-based test runner:** It is allowed to run and debug RSpec, Minitest, Shoulda, and Cucumber tests right from this IDE. The runner will illustrate the whole progress using a tree view for all running tests, including basic data about the status and duration of a particular test.

  You normally generate tests from predefined customizable templates or you can create your own test navigating to it from a class, and replicating the directory structure based on the path to the test subject.

- **Navigate between tests and test subjects:** In addition to the previous point, in RubyMine, you can easily navigate between a test and the test subject. If you are using FactoryBot, you can even navigate from models to factories and vice-versa.

- **View code coverage:** It is allowed to measure how much of your code is covered with tests using integration with SimpleCov. You can also review the percentage of covered files and lines in a separate tool window and editor, as well as generate HTML reports if necessary.

Since RubyMine is a commercial IDE, the price per user is US $199.00.

Home page: https://www.jetbrains.com/ruby/

2. **Sublime Text:** Sublime Text is the code editor that is customizable, user-friendly, and high-performing. It is one of the most popular editors due to its convenient user interface and the capability to add plugins, which can turn it into a fully-featured IDE. Other key features of the editor include the following:

- **Graphics Processing Unit Rendering:** Sublime Text can utilize your graphics processing unit on Linux, Mac, and Windows when rendering the interface. This results in an interactive, vivid user interface all the way up to 8K resolutions, all while taking less power than before.

- **Tab Multi-Select:** File tabs have been upgraded to make split views effortless, with support throughout the whole interface and built-in methods. The sidebar, tab bar, Go to Anything, Go to Definition, auto-complete, and more have all been advanced to make code navigation easier and more intuitive.

- **Context-aware autocomplete:** The auto-complete engine has been modified to provide smart completions based on the existing code library in a project. Suggestions are also reinforced with data about their kind, and additional links to definitions.

- **Enhanced user interface:** The Default and Adaptive themes have been enhanced with new tab styles and inactive pane dimming. Themes and Color Schemes support auto dark-mode switching. The Adaptive theme on Windows and Linux was made to feature custom title bars.

- **Superpowered syntax definitions:** The syntax highlighting engine has been significantly upgraded with new components like handling non-deterministic grammars, multi-line constructs, lazy embeds, and syntax inheritance. In addition, memory usage has been reduced, making load time faster than ever. You can start using the editor at the price of $99 USD.

Home page: https://www.sublimetext.com/

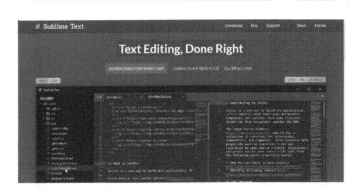

3. **Cloud9:** Cloud9 IDE is an online IDE that supports multiple programming languages, including C, C++, PHP, Ruby, Perl, Python, JavaScript with Node.js, and Go. IDE is scripted almost entirely in JavaScript, using Node.js on the back-end with the Ace editor component.

In 2016 Cloud9 was acquired by Amazon and became a part of Amazon Web Services (AWS). Meaning that as a new user you may only use the Cloud9 service through an AWS account. This IDE presents the development environment for nearly all programming languages comprising Ruby. That is making it very popular amongst medium to big enterprises and companies like Soundcloud and Mozilla, just to name a few already using Cloud9.

You can get the hosted development setting of Ruby on Rails in Cloud9 and retrieve commands just like you would do on your regular workstation. With Cloud9 you get practically all the characteristics that you require for Ruby on Rails development including a text editor, file manager, Unix shell, preview, and chatting for team collaboration. Other essential features include the following:

- It supplies a browser-based editor that enables simple scripting, running, and debugging of your projects. The themes for the editor you can choose yourself.

- It encompasses the integrated panel debugger that assists in breakpoint, check variables state and the whole code.

- It enables you to activate commands, such as compiling your code, forward code changes to git, and display command output from servers.

- Tools, namely Serverless Application Model (SAM), use templates in Cloud9 to deliver a streamlined way of describing resources for any serverless applications.

- Moreover, as an online IDE, Cloud9 allows simultaneous editing from multiple users by offering a variety of different cursors and can support the creation of private and public projects. Users can also drag-and-drop files into projects and use tabs to organize multiple files.

- Cloud9 has a built-in terminal, with npm and basic Unix commands.

- Built-in Image Editor.

- It is also popular for its support for deployment to Heroku, Joyent, Microsoft Azure, Google App Engine, and SFTP/FTP.

Even though it is technically a commercial tool, it still has certain free tier offers that do not expire and are available to all AWS customers:

- **12 months free:** Meaning that you can enjoy Cloud9 for 12-months following your initial sign-up date to AWS.

- **Pay-as-you-go:** This option allows you to adapt to changing business needs without overcommitting budgets and reducing the risk of overprovisioning or missing capacity.

- **Save when you commit:** This saving plan offers usage and payment On-Demand in exchange for a commitment to use a specific amount (measured in $/hour) of an AWS service or a category of services, for a one- or three-year period.

- **Payless by using more:** Here, you can get volume-based discounts and realize important savings as your usage increases. For services such as Cloud9, pricing is tiered, meaning the more you use, the less you pay.

Home page: https://aws.amazon.com/?nc2=h_lg

FREE IDE OPTIONS

Nowadays most modern IDE offer intelligent code completion. The IDE design support programmer by advancing the productivity with tight-knit components that have a somewhat similar user interface that allow them to easily use them. Some IDEs have either a compiler or an interpreter such as SharpDevelop and Lazarus. While some other IDE such as NetBeans and Eclipse have both the compiler and interpreter for the execution of code. Some IDEs are mainly designed for a specific programming language. However, there are many multiple-language IDE that let users complete programming for multiple languages using just one open-source IDE. We shall go through such in this section.

1. **Aptana:** Aptana Studio is one of the most popular open-source IDEs out there that help to make dynamic programming web applications. Aptana Studio provides integrated support with Rails and is therefore considered the best IDE for Ruby on Rails

owing to its usage of the external plugin RadRails, which includes a lot of high-tech features to simplify the development of database-driven web apps. Additionally, this tool has upgrading novel features to advance productivity and enable customization. Some other key features are:

- **HTML, CSS, and JavaScript Code Assist:** Aptana is great at helping to authorize HTML, CSS, JavaScript, and PHP. It supports the latest HTML specifications and includes data about the level of support for each element in major web browsers.

- **Deployment Wizard:** This IDE offers support for one-shot as well as keep-synchronized setup using multiple protocols including FTP, SFTP, FTPS, and Capistrano. It also has a great ability to automatically present your Rails applications to hosting services such as Heroku or Engine Yard.

- **Integrated Debugger:** With the Integrated Debugger feature, you can set breakpoints, inspect variables, and control the whole implementation. The integrated Rails and JavaScript debuggers can also help you to get rid of any bugs.

- **Git Integration:** With Aptana, you can easily put your projects under git source code control and collaborate with team members through the merge, pull and push options to access remote repositories such as those located in Github.

- **Built-in Terminal:** It is possible to quickly access a command line terminal for the implementation of operating system commands and language utilities such as gem or rake.

- **IDE Customization:** You can set up your development environment precisely the way you want it by extending the core capabilities by adding certain custom commands. Aptana has hundreds of commands that could be easily accessed depending on the type of file you are editing.

Home page: http://www.aptana.com/

2. **NetBeans:** NetBeans IDE is one of the most used IDE for various programming languages. It is a smarter way to code for programmers as it allows users to quickly and easily create desktop, mobile, and web apps not only with Rails but also with Java, HTML 5, PHP, and C/C++. Just like previous IDEs, it is available for free with a big community of users and developers.

NetBeans is applied for diverse programming languages as a prevalent IDE for development. It is considered a faster way for developers to code as it offers end-to-end app development traits, continuously improving Java Editor, maintaining frequent speed, and performance enhancements. With that, it is safe to say that NetBeans IDE sets the benchmark for application development.

Naturally, NetBeans arises from Oracle and relishes the support of a huge community of users and developers. Some of its key features include:

- It is the first IDE to support the newest versions of the Java EE, JDK, and JavaFX.

- It is cross-platform and runs on Windows, Linux, macOS, and Solaris.

- It provides smart outlines to help you comprehend and manage your applications, containing great support for popular modern technologies.

Home page: https://netbeans.apache.org/

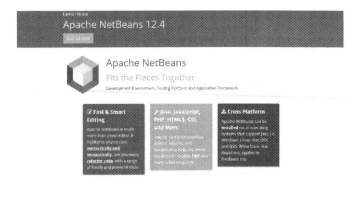

3. **Vim:** Vim is another open-source, free-to-use text editor for Ruby on Rails that is considered to be rich in features. It is keyboard-based, which can make moving from file to file quickly. It is also accessible as the best Ruby IDE for Linux with plugins that present a choice to convert this text editor into an influential Ruby development environment. Essential V plugins include:

- **NERDTree:** used to navigate the file tree.

- **FZF:** let you complete search through the files in the project

- **jiangmiao/auto-pairs:** used to insert quotes and parenthesis in pairs as you script

- **tpope/vim-commentary:** applied to comment out a line or a selection in visual mode.

As well as that, outstanding Vim features include the following:

- **Syntax highlighting:** It offers decent syntax highlighting for Ruby files out of the box. You may also use a custom highlighter for certain template formats, for instance, SLIM.

- **Linting:** One of the main things your text editor should do for you is linting: spotting your syntax errors, and helping you fix them. Let us see briefly how you can get yourself an optimal linting experience in Vim.

For linting in Vim, it is recommended to use a plugin called ALE. Basically, it runs an external linter for you asynchronously so it does not block the user interface. ALE is a great plugin and supports plenty of languages and linters. So if you have it installed in the system it will run the current file for you, so you do not have to set up anything. Although if you need to specify which linters you want to run, you can do this in the settings file by providing the following variable:[1]

```
let g:ale_linters = {
        \   'ruby': ['standardrb',
'rubocop'],
        \   'python': ['flake8', 'pylint'],
        \   'javascript': ['eslint'],
        \}
```

In order to review the full list of available linters for the current file, you can run :ALEInfo<Enter> in the command line. Some of those linters can also fix your code. For instance, testdouble/standard can both fix the errors and format the file. In order to set it up for your file there is another variable you need to insert:

```
let g:ale_fixers = {
        \    'ruby': ['standardrb'],
        \}
let g:ale_fix_on_save = 1
```

The last line of the code above is a great time saver – it will automatically fix and thus format your file on save.

---

[1] https://www.vimfromscratch.com/articles/vim-for-ruby-and-rails-in-2019/, Vimfromscratch

There is another convenient configuration option that illustrates the total number of warnings and errors in the status line:[2]

```
function! LinterStatus() abort
  let l:counts =
ale#statusline#Count(bufnr(''))
  let l:all_errors = l:counts.error +
l:counts.style_error
  let l:all_non_errors = l:counts.total
- l:all_errors

  return l:counts.total == 0?  '  all good
 ' : printf(
        \   '  %dW %dE',
        \   all_non_errors,
        \   all_errors
        \)
endfunction

set statusline=
set statusline+=%m
set statusline+=\ %f
set statusline+=%=
set statusline+=\ %{LinterStatus()}
```

In case you decide that ALE is not your cup of tea, here are a couple of alternatives to look at:

- **vim-syntastic/syntastic:** very popular one but synchronous which can cause significant delays in the user interface.

---

[2] https://www.vimfromscratch.com/articles/vim-for-ruby-and-rails-in-2019/, Vimfromscratch

- **neomake/neomake:** asynchronous linting that is used to build a framework for Neovim code editor.

- **Navigation between files:** It often happens that you would want to quickly jump from one file to another (for instance, from a model to controller, or from the controller to test). This is what Vim Rails lets you do. It offers plugins that enhance your Rails code and enable you to do complete things like:

  - Use Emodel, :Eview, :Econtroller to easily jump to corresponding model, view and any controller files.

  - Offers :Rails runner execution

  - Use :Rails without arguments to activate the test, specification, or feature

  - Autocompletion

Autocompletion in dynamic languages like Ruby could be challenging at times. But Vim can definitely help with that by indexing and analyzing large chunks of data files. Now, how to set and modify the autocomplete function exactly? First and foremost, it is recommended to install the deoplete plugin which acts like an asynchronous completion framework that suggests completion options for you as you type. To enable it, insert the following:

```
let g:deoplete#enable_at_startup = 1
```

Or you can also get it through this Tab code:

```
inoremap <silent><expr> <TAB>
      \ pumvisible()?  "\<C-n>" :
      \ <SID>check_back_space()?  "\<TAB>" :
      \
deoplete#mappings#manual_complete()
function! s:check_back_space() abort "{{{
  let col = col('.') - 1
  return !col || getline('.')[col - 1]  =~ '\s'
endfunction"}}}
```

Additionally, there is another concept called "Language Servers" first introduced by Microsoft with TypeScript which denotes a separate process running in the background and analyzing your code as you type. Editors and IDEs can communicate with this process and ask for some specific information like syntax errors or autocomplete suggestions. You can unlock such feature on Rails as well by using the following gem:

```
gem install solargraph
solargraph socket
```

Then you will also need a Language Server plugin for Vim. In order for it to work you need to tell it where it should find the language server for a particular language. For that, insert the following into your vim settings:

```
let g:LanguageClient_serverCommands = {
    \ 'ruby': ['~/.rbenv/shims/solargraph',
'stdio'],
    \ }
```

With that, restart Vim and see if you can use it. Additionally, for better Rails support you might also want to run:

```
solargraph bundle
```

This will manage multiple operational tasks in the background for you as well as enable you to autocomplete things like belongs_to, before_action, and other Rails-specific methods.

In case the original deoplete plugin would seem on the harder side for you, it is possible to check the following alternatives:

- **YouCompleteMe:** an older code-completion engine with a great rating on GitHub.

- **SuperTab:** another Vim plugin that you can use for many insert completion needs.

- **Expanding:** By Expanding we mean expanding a snippet with the Neosnippet Vim plugin. Snippet stands for the capacity to script something short then have it expanded into a full method where you can insert the method name right away and then move to the code body. As usual, there are several engines that can do the trick for you, but a slight challenge here is how to actually make it compatible with other plugins you already have, like auto-completion plugins.

In case you are using the previously mentioned deoplete plugin for completion, then it is recommended to try the Neosnippet Vim plugin for expanding:

```
if has('nvim')
  Plug 'Shougo/deoplete.nvim', { 'do':
':UpdateRemotePlugins' }
```

```
else
  Plug 'Shougo/deoplete.nvim'
  Plug 'roxma/nvim-yarp'
  Plug 'roxma/vim-hug-neovim-rpc'
endif

Plug 'Shougo/neosnippet.vim'
Plug 'Shougo/neosnippet-snippets'
```

Certain mappings might be helpful as well:
```
imap <C-k>    <Plug>(neosnippet_expand_
or_jump)
smap <C-k>    <Plug>(neosnippet_expand_or_
jump)
xmap <C-k>    <Plug>(neosnippet_expand_
target)
```

With all the above code you can activate a snippet through the familiar deoplete interface, and then press <C-k> multiple times to expand the snippet and move the cursor to the next editable part.

Home page: https://www.vim.org/

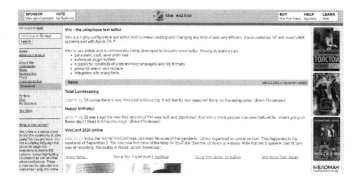

4. **Atom:** Atom editor is an open-source IDE from Github, now a subsidiary of Microsoft, that is known for its extremely customizable traits that simplify code development.

Atom is also great for increasing productivity without moving the configuration file each time. Typically, it does not operate on its own since it gets support from the Github seamless practice. With Atom you can create new branches, set and commit, push and pull, resolve merge conflicts, view pull requests, and more – all from within your editor. And since the GitHub package is already bundled with Atom, it supports numerous programming languages that include Ruby. Some other features of Atom for Rails development are:

- **Cross-platform editing:** Atom works across operating systems and you can use it on OS X, Windows, or Linux.

- **Built-in package manager:** You can search for and install new packages or create your own right from Atom.

- **Smart autocompletion:** Atom lets you write code faster with a smart and fast autocomplete feature.

- **File system browser:** With a File system browser you can easily browse and open a single file, a whole project, or multiple projects in one window.

- **Multiple panes:** This particular feature allows you to split your Atom interface into multiple panes to compare and edit code across files.

- **Find and replace:** With Atom you can find, preview, and replace any text as you type in a file or across all your projects.

- **Themes:** Atom comes pre-installed with four user interface options and eight syntax themes in both dark and light colors. And if you still cannot find what would suit you perfectly, then it is possible to install themes created by experts of the Atom community or even create your own.

- **Customization:** It is very easy to customize and style Atom. You can change or completely reset the look and feel of your interface with CSS/Less, and add major features with HTML and JavaScript.

- **Under the hood:** Atom was initially built with HTML, JavaScript, CSS, and Node.js integration. And it runs on Electron, a framework for creating cross-platform applications using web technologies.

Home page: https://atom.io/

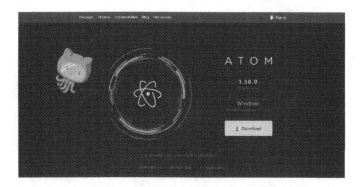

5. **Emacs:** Emacs is preferred by many multifunctional editors for Ruby and Ruby on Rails-based web programming. It is free to use and can be modified and customized as per your many requirements. Emacs is heavily utilized by Rails community developers, and for that reason, there are a devoted Rails plugins like ruby-tools, rubocop-emacs, rake, rvm, chruby, bundler, and rbenv.named that enhance Ruby mode for supporting Rails programming. Other important Emacs features include:

- Content-aware editing modes, including syntax coloring for many file types.

- Complete built-in documentation, including a tutorial for new users.

- Full Unicode support for nearly all code scripts.

- Highly customizable Emacs Lisp code and a graphical user interface.

- A wide range of functionality including a project planner, mail and newsreader, debugger interface, calendar, and Internet Relay Chat client.

- Default packaging system for downloading and installing extensions.

Additionally, the Emacs Project also has a very interesting philosophy that they manifest to it user community that is based on the concept of freedom software. Free software means that the software's users have freedom. Professionals developed the Emacs tool so that users can have freedom in their computing.

To be precise, the statement also explains that[3]

> free software means users have the four essential freedoms: (0) to run the program, (1) to study and change the program in source code form, (2) to redistribute exact copies, and (3) to distribute modified versions. Software differs from material objects – such as chairs, sandwiches, and gasoline – in that it can be copied and changed much more easily. These facilities are why software is useful; we believe a program's users should be free to take advantage of them, not solely its developer.

As a beginner, you are certainly going to devote much of your time to opt for the required EDI for your web development project. Therefore, it is crucial to have a tool that you are comfortable and most productive with. Most of the IDEs mentioned above for Rails development are either free or give a free trial version. It is always helpful to try out a few of them before you decide which one to stick with. Here are certain things that you should consider before selecting the best text editor for Ruby:

First, look at inbuilt characteristics that promise to enhance your productivity like auto-complete, code snippets, and clean design that does not get in your way. See whether the selected Ruby on Rails IDE is open-source or not. Also, make sure to double-check what Ruby-related plugins are accessible to create things easier and increase your productivity in building applications.

Home page: https://www.gnu.org/software/emacs/

---

[3] https://www.gnu.org/savannah-checkouts/gnu/emacs/emacs.html#features, Gnu

MIDDLEMAN GENERATOR

Middleman is a static site generator that uses all the short-cuts and tools of modern web development. It shares many conventions with Ruby on Rails making it familiar and feasible to migrate to Rails if that need ever arises.

In the last few years we have seen an explosion in the amount and variety of tools developers can utilize to create web applications. Ruby on Rails selects a handful of these tools such:

- Sass for DRY stylesheets
- CoffeeScript for safe and fluid Javascript
- Multiple asset management solutions, including Sprockets
- ERb & Haml for dynamic pages and simplified HTML syntax

Additionally, many websites are built with an API in mind. Instead of packaging the frontend and the backend together, both can be built and deployed independently using the public API to pull data from the backend and show it on the frontend. Static websites are incredibly fast and require very little memory space. A front-end built to stand-alone can be deployed directly to the cloud or a Content Delivery Network. Many developers choose to simply deliver static HTML/JS/CSS to their clients.

Middleman is distributed using the RubyGems package manager. This means you will require both the Ruby language runtime installed and RubyGems to start using Middleman. macOS comes prepackaged with both Ruby and RubyGems, yet some of the Middleman's dependencies have to be compiled during installation and on macOS that requires Xcode Command Line Tools. Xcode can be installed from the terminal:

```
$ xcode-select --install
```

Once you have Ruby and RubyGems up and running, implement the following from the command line:

```
$ gem install middleman
```

This feature installs Middleman, its dependencies, and the command-line tools for using Middleman. This installation process also adds the following three useful features:

```
$ middleman init
$ middleman server
$ middleman build
```

Once you are done with the installation, you need to get started and create a project folder for Middleman to work out of. You can complete this using an existing folder or have Middleman create one for you using the middleman init command:

- **$ middleman init:** builds a Middleman skeleton project in your current folder.

- **$ middleman init my_new_project:** creates a subfolder my_new_project with the Middleman skeleton project.

The Skeleton

Every new project you start provides a basic web development skeleton for you. This automates the building of a standard hierarchy of folders and files that you can apply in all of your projects. A brand-new project must typically have a source folder and a config.rb file. The source folder is where you will build your website. Additionally, the skeleton project has JavaScript, CSS, and images folders, but you can change these to serve your own personal preferences.

Gemfile

Middleman uses a Bundler Gemfile for identifying and controlling your gem dependencies. When working on a new project, Middleman will generate a Gemfile for you which uses the same version of Middleman you are working with, locking Middleman to this specific release series. All plugins and extra libraries you use in your project should be listed in your Gemfile, and Middleman will automatically request all of them when it starts running.

config.ru

A config.ru file is used to define how the site would be loaded by a Rack-enabled web server. If you would like to host your Middleman site in development mode on a Rack-based host such as Heroku, you can add a config.ru file at the root of your project with the following code:

```
require 'middleman/rack'
run Middleman.server
```

At the same time, keep in mind that Middleman is built to generate static sites and this scenario is not a primary use-case.

At last, when you are ready to deliver static code or host a static blog, you will need to build the site. Using the command-line, from the project folder, you are expected to run middleman build:

```
$ cd my_project
$ bundle exec middleman build
```

This will create a static file for each file located in your source folder. Afterward, template files will be compiled, static files will be copied and any enabled build-time features (such as compression) will be implemented. Middleman will as well automatically remove all the unnecessary files from the build directory for you so they do not get involved with the production.

In order to speed up the build time, you can expose the variable NO_CONTRACTS=true like that:

```
$ cd my_project
$ NO_CONTRACTS=true bundle exec middleman
build
```

Contracts like the above one, are normally used to add type signatures to certain methods, and Middleman utilizes them internally to override and remove the gems' classes, so no type checking is necessary.

After building the site you are supposed to have everything you need within the build directory. There are multiple ways to deploy a static build. So we only present one solution for this, but you should feel free to search the web or look at the extension directory for more alternatives to deploy Middleman. If you are an author of a deployment tool suitable to deploy Middleman, you may open a pull request to the directory. A very convenient tool to deploy a build is middleman-deploy. It can deploy a site via Rsync, FTP, SFTP, or Git:

```
$ middleman build [--clean]
$ middleman deploy [--build-before]
```

Production Asset Hashing

A standard setup for production is to hash your assets and serve them through a Content Delivery Network. You can accomplish this easily with Middleman:[4]

```
configure :build do
  activate :minify_css
  activate :minify_javascript

  # Append a hash to asset urls (make sure
to use the url helpers)
  activate :asset_hash
```

---

[4] https://middlemanapp.com/basics/build-and-deploy/, Middleman

```
  activate :asset_host, :host => '//
YOURDOMAIN.cloudfront.net'
end
```

Templates

Middleman provides access to many templating languages to ease your HTML development. The languages range from simply letting you use Ruby variables and loops in your pages, to providing a completely different format to script your pages in which compiles to HTML. Moreover, Middleman has built-in support for the Haml, Sass, SCSS, and CoffeeScript engines (more engines can be enabled by including their Tilt-enabled gems).

However, the default templating language for Middleman is ERB. ERB looks similar to the HTML, except it lets you insert variables, call methods, and use loops and if statements. Generally, all of the template files in Middleman include the extension of the ERB in their filename. A simple index page written in ERB would be named index.html. erb which includes the full filename, index.html, and the ERB extension.

File Size Optimization

Middleman can as well handle CSS minification and JavaScript compression so you do not have to worry about it. Most libraries provide minified and compressed versions of their files for users to deploy, but these files could be unreadable or editable. Middleman allows you to keep the original, commented files in the project so you can easily read them and modify if needed. Then, when you build the project, Middleman will manage all the optimization for you.

To start with, in your config.rb, you are expected to activate the minify_css and minify_javascript features during the build of your site:

```
configure :build do
  activate :minify_css
  activate :minify_javascript
end
```

In case you are already using a compressed file that includes .min in its filename, Middleman will not feature it. This could be a great option for libraries like jQuery which are carefully compressed by their authors ahead of time.

It is also possible to customize how the JavaScript compressor operates by setting the :compressor option for the :minify_javascript extension in config.rb to a custom instance of Uglifier. To illustrate with an example, you could enable unsafe optimizations and mangle top-level variable names like this:

```
require "uglifier"
activate :minify_javascript,
  compressor: proc {
    ::Uglifier.new(:mangle => {:toplevel
=> true}, :compress => {:unsafe => true})
  }
```

In case you have asset_hash activated, make sure that you keep mangling variables disabled at the same time. If mangling is enabled, Uglifier will create different compressed versions of the JavaScript on each machine, resulting in different hashes in the filename and different references in each version of the HTML. For instance:

```
require "uglifier"
activate :minify_javascript, compressor:
-> { Uglifier.new(:mangle => false) }
```

However, in case you need to exclude any files from being minified, pass the :ignore option when activating these extensions, and give it one or more globs, regexes, or procs that mark the files to ignore. Likewise, you can pass an :exts option to show which file extensions are renamed.

If you want to speed up your JavaScript minification (and CoffeeScript builds), you can do it by including these gems in your Gemfile:

```
gem 'therubyracer' # faster JS compiles
gem 'oj' # faster JSON parser and object
serializer
gzip text files
```

It is also recommended to serve compressed files to user agents that can manage them. Many web servers have the ability to gzip files on the go, but that requires Central Processing Unit work every time the file is served, and as a result, most servers cannot complete the maximum compression. Middleman can produce gzipped versions of your HTML, CSS, and JavaScript alongside your regular files, and you can instruct your webserver to serve those pre-gzipped files directly. For that, you need to enable the :gzip extension first:

```
activate :gzip
```

Then if you want to compress images on build, you can try middleman-imageoptim. Middleman also provides an official extension for minifying its HTML output. Simply add middleman-minify-HTML to your Gemfile:

```
gem "middleman-minify-HTML"
```

After that run bundle installs, open your config.rb and insert:

```
activate :minify_html
```

As a result, you should see view-source:'ing that your HTML is now being minified.

Custom Extensions

Middleman extensions are Ruby classes that can connect to various points of the Middleman system, add new features and modify content. The following sections will explain some of what is available, but it is also advised to additionally access the Middleman source and the source of plugins like middleman-blog to browse all the hooks and extension options.

In order to establish a new extension, you can use the standard extension command. This will create all needed files:[5]

```
middleman extension middleman-my_extension
# create  middleman-my_extension/.gitignore
# create  middleman-my_extension/Rakefile
```

---

[5] https://middlemanapp.com/advanced/custom-extensions/, Middleman

```
# create  middleman-my_extension/
middleman-my_extension.gemspec
# create  middleman-my_extension/Gemfile
# create  middleman-my_extension/lib/
middleman-my_extension/extension.rb
# create  middleman-my_extension/lib/
middleman-my_extension.rb
# create  middleman-my_extension/features/
support/env.rb
# create  middleman-my_extension/fixtures
```

Basic Extension

At the same time, the most basic extension looks like:

```
class MyFeature < Middleman::Extension
  def initialize(app, options_hash={}, &block)
    super
  end
  alias :included :registered
end
::Middleman::Extensions.register(:my_
feature, MyFeature)
```

The above module should be kept accessible to your config. rb file. So you should either define it directly in that file or define it in another Ruby file and require it in config.rb Finally, once your module is included, you must activate it in config.rb using the following feature:

```
activate :my_feature
```

The register method lets you choose the name your extension is activated with. It can also take a block if you want to require files only when your extension is activated.

In the MyFeature extension, the initialize method will be called as soon as the activate command is run. The app variable is an instance of Middleman::Application class.

activate can also take an options hash (which are passed to register) or a block that can be used to configure your extension. You define options with the options class method and then access them with the following variable:[6]

```ruby
class MyFeature < Middleman::Extension
    option :foo, false, 'Controls whether
we foo'
  def initialize(app, options_hash={},
&block)
    super
    puts options.foo
  end
end
```

Adding Methods to config.rb

Methods within your extension can be made available to config.rb through the following expose_to_config method:

```ruby
class MyFeature < Middleman::Extension
  expose_to_config :say_hello
  def say_hello
    puts "Hello"
  end
end
```

---

[6] https://middlemanapp.com/advanced/custom-extensions/, Middleman

Similar to config, methods can be added to any Middleman template context:

```
class MyFeature < Middleman::Extension
  expose_to_template :say_hello
  def say_hello
    "Hello Template"
  end
end
```

Adding Helpers

Another way to add methods to templates is by using helpers. Unlike exposed methods from before, helpers do not have access to the whole extension. They are mostly preferred for bigger sets of methods combined into a module. In other cases, the above-exposed methods are preferred. You can activate helpers with the following code:

```
class MyFeature < Middleman::Extension
  def initialize(app, options_hash={},
&block)
    super
  end

  helpers do
    def make_a_link(url, text)
      "<a href='#{url}'>#{text}</a>"
    end
  end
end
```

Now, with helpers inside your templates, you will have access to a make_a_link method.

Sitemap Manipulators

It is also possible to modify or add pages in the sitemap by creating a Sitemap extension. The directory_indexes extension uses this feature to reroute standard pages to their directory-index version, and the blog extension uses several plugins to create a tag and calendar pages. As an example of sitemap manipulators we shall illustrate the manipulate_resource_list that is required to return the full set of resources to be passed to the next step of the pipeline:

```
class MyFeature < Middleman::Extension
  def manipulate_resource_list(resources)
    resources.each do |resource|
      resource.destination_path.
gsub!("original", "new")
    end

    resources
  end
end
```

Callbacks

At the same time, there are many parts of the Middleman life-cycle that can be accessed by various extensions. For example, at times when you want to wait until the config .rb has been executed to run code and for that, you rely on the :css_dir variable, waiting until it has been set. To unlock and manipulate this process, you can use this callback:[7]

---

[7] https://middlemanapp.com/advanced/custom-extensions/, Middleman

after_configuration

```
class MyFeature < Middleman::Extension
  def after_configuration
    puts app.config[:css_dir]
  end
end
```

after_build

This callback is applied to implement code after the build process has been completed. The middleman-smusher extension uses this feature to compress all the image files in the build folder after it has been created. It is also possible to integrate a deployment script after build:

```
class MyFeature < Middleman::Extension
  def after_build(builder)
    builder.thor.run './my_deploy_script.sh'
  end
end
```

There are also additionally available callbacks such as the following:[8]

- **initialized:** called before config is parsed, and before extensions are registered

- **configure:** called to run any configure blocks for the current environment or the current mode

- **before_extensions:** called before the ExtensionManager is activated

---

[8] https://middlemanapp.com/advanced/custom-extensions/, Middleman

- **before_instance_block:** called before any blocks are passed to the configuration context

- **before_sitemap:** called before the SiteMap::Store is activated, which initializes the sitemap

- **before_configuration:** called before configuration is parsed, mostly used for extensions

- **after_configuration_eval:** called after the configuration is parsed, before the pre-extension callback

- **ready:** called when everything is stable

- **before_build:** called before the site build process runs

- **before_shutdown:** called in the shutdown! method used to notify users that the application is shutting down

- **before:** called before Rack requests

- **before_server:** called before the PreviewServer is produced

- **reload:** called before the new application is initialized on a reload event

To conclude, Middleman is a rich and ever-evolving tool that definitely deserves to be studied and applied on any project basis. All of the updates and system changes can be tracked through social media, you just need to search and follow @middlemanapp tag in whatever platform you are on.

Appraisal

Ruby on Rails is an open-source software used to create web applications. Rails stands for a framework based on the general-purpose programming language Ruby that ranks amongst the top programming languages predominantly because of Rails popularity.

It is normal for a developer to look for ways that help in reducing the amount of effort and time put into building a web application, something that can automate the tedious tasks that are involved in the process of creating a website. Ruby on Rails is just the software for that. It is manageable, user-friendly, and designed on the Model-View-Controller (MVC) architecture that offers numerous benefits.

Whether you have been programming for years and want to give web development in Ruby a try, or you are a complete coding newbie wanting to see if programming is for you, Rails is a great tool to learn. Most of the resources in this book assume no programming knowledge – more advanced readers may choose to skim the introductory sections of each to learn the particulars of Ruby and Rails.

DOI: 10.1201/9781003229605-7

As already mentioned, Rails is designed on the basic MVC software design pattern for developing web applications. It is made up of three parts:

1. **Modal:** It is the lowest level of the pattern that is responsible for maintaining data.

2. **View:** It is accountable for displaying a portion of or all data to the viewer.

3. **Controller:** It is the software code that administers interactions between Modal and View.

MVC detaches the application logic from the user interface layer and assists the severance of concerns. The controller is the center that receives the requests for the application and then performs with Modal to generate the required results which are then in turn displayed by View. Due to these Ruby on Rails' building features, it is usually applied for creating Software as a service (Saas) solutions. It is also beneficial to use Ruby on Rails to create Social Networking sites or any other non-standard complex projects.

From the business perspective, Ruby on Rails has many different advantages:

- **Easy to manage changes:** Ruby on Rails makes it easy to optimize the existing code or add new features to the site. After site launch, future editions to your site (like making any remarkable changes to the data model) are simple and fast to complete. This is particularly most convenient for long-term projects due to its stability and precision.

- **Secure:** Some security measures are included in the framework and activated by default. Using Ruby on Rails, you would follow the secure development life-cycle, which might be a complicated security assurance approach. But Rails community constantly works to spot and fix new vulnerabilities and the framework is well documented by its dedicated users.

  For applications with lots of functions and data handling, Rails could slow the application down. If this is often happening in your application, you could always opt for code optimization, which greatly improves performance outcomes.

- **Flexibility:** Web applications use the frontend and backend capabilities of Rails because these are simpler and easier to create. Yet the application needs to communicate with the server to load the webpage and can lack the immediate responsiveness to a user's taps and selections.

  Single page web applications can be more complicated to create but may allow for more involved user interfaces and provide instant responses to user's actions by only loading some parts of the website as needed. A single-page web application would usually use something like Angular or React for the frontend. However, it would still use Rails as a backend, allowing your application to rely on some of Rails best features.

- **Productivity:** Ruby is a concise language, and when combined with third-party libraries, it lets you develop features especially fast. It is one of the most productive programming languages around. Nearly all of these libraries are released in the form of a gem, a packaged library, or an application that can be installed with a specific Ruby plugin.

- **A large repository of free plugins:** The abundance of free plugins is another great Rails advantage. In operating with Rails, you can customize your website for any organizational need – for instance, create your own exclusive social network or launch advanced e-commerce services with a high level of user data protection.

On the other hand, there are certain Rails disadvantages that one should be aware of:

- **Runtime Speed:** One of the areas of concern is slow runtime speed. It is true that other top environments and frameworks (like Node.js or Django) are somewhat faster than Rails. Twitter, for instance, decided to boost Rails performance that decreased after the social network became highly popular, by replacing certain internal communication components and server daemons with Scala solutions.

- **Boot Speed:** Boot speed can also affect the developer's time. Depending on the number of plugin dependencies and files, it can take a significant amount of time to start. At the same time, one should take not solely development and design into consideration. Some maintenance, debugging, and adding new functions should take a longer time. Be prepared for that and you might avoid plenty of issues in the future.

With the current variety of programming languages, frameworks, platforms, and development environments that we have nowadays, one cannot go without comparing one to the other. Rails is often correlated to other frameworks and environments due to its multi-capacity and flexibility. It tends to completely cross the line that distinguishes conventional categories like languages and frameworks, providing a handful of tools to complete scalable and high-quality work.

- **Ruby on Rails vs Python:** Python is a general-purpose programming language. Some perceive Python as an all-purpose language that is able to meet any requirements of the coder without having to look for any external tools. In contrast to Python, Ruby on Rails is not a language, it stands out as a framework built upon the Ruby language and explicitly used for web development.

- **Ruby on Rails vs PHP:** PHP is a language with an object-oriented programming (OOP) structure used for coding. It is mostly applied in software development, while Rails is the framework sought for web development. Same as with Python, this comparison with PHP would not be entirely correct since Ruby on Rails is not a language. However, you most likely going to experience many situations where Ruby on Rails and PHP would be applied within the same project.

- **Ruby on Rails vs Java:** Java is one of the oldest and widely popular languages. It is specifically known as a language to create applications for a variety of operating systems. This technology is especially well-known as being a top language for developing Android apps. In contrast to Java, Rails is mostly applied for web development purposes.

- **Ruby on Rails vs JavaScript:** Although they are similarly named, Java and Javascript are completely different scripting languages that were made for different purposes. Java's goal is to enable developers to apply the same code on different operating systems without having to optimize it much. Yet nowadays, Java applets are getting less popular, with most users preferring Java support disabled in their browsers. On the other hand, Javascript is more popular than ever as it runs perfectly well with modern web browsers, especially on mobile.

Moreover, JavaScript is one of the most widely-used front-end programming languages, particularly focused on creating versatile user interfaces for web applications for different devices. Rails and Java share a few basic similarities, but for the most part, they should be perceived as completely different languages. They are both strongly-typed and OOP languages, but Rails is an interpreted scripting language while Java is a compiled coding language.

JavaScript and Ruby on Rails are both in high demand right now, and both are viewed as lucrative web development programming languages that have apparent advantages. At the same time, they go hand in hand really well. That is why, if presented with a choice whether to learn Ruby or Javascript, you should consider taking the third option and learn both of these computer programming languages.

- **Ruby on Rails vs Node.js:** Node.js is an open-source platform for implementing JavaScript code server-side, as it was primarily built on the JavaScript runtime. Fundamentally, you should not be comparing Node.JS to Rails at all since unlike Rails, Node is not a framework but an application runtime environment that enables scripting on the server-side application using Javascript, while Ruby on Rails is a full-featured framework.

Nevertheless, in order to discuss Rails and its relevance for beginners, it is important to take a step back and understand that it is not just the Rails framework that is beginner-friendly, but the Ruby language it is founded on as well. Basically, Rails IS Ruby, or at least it exists on top of Ruby. This means that learning Rails will involve reviewing at least some parts of the Ruby programming language – though nothing beyond simple syntax.

The Ruby language itself – and not just the Rails web framework – is a great choice as a beginning coding language – it is easy to read and does a lot of the work for you. Other languages, like C, require a lot more code to complete something you can achieve in a few lines with Ruby. And since Rails is like an extension of Ruby, you can truly master Ruby on Rails once you have learned Ruby variables, blocks, comments, and key control structures.

When you are creating an app with Ruby on Rails development, chances are, you will have to manage the massive amount of data. And in a project as such, without a solid data structure, it will quickly become a mad clutter. Especially if you are building a backend in Ruby on Rails, creating a database that will take care of data-based processes and keep the app's information structured is essential. Therefore, this book also includes a chapter about the most popular databases in Ruby on Rails web development, introducing you to the process of consolidating them and outlining the best practices.

Simply put, Ruby on Rails is a Web application framework made for developing Web applications. And in your application, if you expect or need a user to enter information through a Web form, you require a database to store all that information. In Rails framework, the database table has a plural name (ending with "s"), and the primary key in the database is known as id and auto-incremented. To retrieve stored information from the database, Rails utilizes a component named ActiveRecord that operates as a bridge between the database and Ruby code.

If you find yourself in charge of a Rails app for the first time, there are a couple of areas where you really do not want to have any issues:

- **Data Integrity:** Is all the data in your database reliable?

- **Database Performance:** Do your queries return in an appropriate amount of time?

As far as these points are concerned, database transactions (and their ActiveRecord counterparts) are great tools for avoiding these problems. Transactions are typically used when you need to ensure data integrity, even if your web app crashes in the middle of a request. Properly applied, they can speed queries and guarantee data safety.

It is a fact that every project is standardized and set to abide by the same coding practices and flow. Rails is mostly preferred for rapid application development, as this framework offers almost effortless accommodation of any alterations. Rails also has built a particular emphasis on testing and has a sufficient testing framework. Owing to these attributes, the framework is mainly applied by start-ups and businesses who prioritize quick and secure results.

There are many pieces to understand when building web applications, and chances are it might get a bit blurry the first time founding concepts are introduced. This Rails Mastering also makes sure to focus on some additional topics, and if they overlap, hearing the same thing explained two different ways will only make it clearer. This book should be viewed as your primary guide and initial encounter with Ruby in Rails. You now hold all the information necessary to begin with your creations.

Index

Printed in the United States
by Baker & Taylor Publisher Services